Letts

KS3
Success

Revision Guide

Mathematics
SATs
Levels 3-6

Fiona C. Mapp

Contents

Number

Algebra

Shape, space and measures

Handling data

Numbers 1

Place value in whole numbers

Each digit in a number has a **place value**.
The size of the number depends on its place value.
The place value changes by a factor of 10 as you **move** from one column to the next.

These gaps make big
numbers easier to read.

40
↑
The place value is ten
for this digit 4.

ten millions	millions	hundred thousands	ten thousands	thousands	hundreds	tens	units	
						6	2	sixty-two
					5	3	8	five hundred and thirty-eight
				4	2	9	2	four thousand, two hundred and ninety-two
			5	3	4	0	0	fifty-three thousand, four hundred
		2	3	6	5	2	0	two hundred and thirty-six thousand, five hundred and twenty
	4	3	9	5	0	2	5	four million, three hundred and ninety-five thousand and twenty-five

Always read the numbers from left to right.

Ordering whole numbers

- When putting numbers into order of size, it is a good idea to group the numbers with the same number of digits together.
- For each group, arrange the numbers in order of size depending on the place value of the digits.

Example
Arrange these numbers in order of size, smallest first.
  26, 502, 794, 3627, 4209, 4390, 7, 86, 28, 114

This becomes:
  7, 26, 28, 86, 114, 502, 794, 3627, 4209, 4390

Practise your multiplication tables
and ask a friend to test you.

Multiples and odd and even numbers

Odd and even numbers

Every whole number is either **odd** or **even**.

1 2 3 4 5 6 7 8 9 10 11 12 13 14 15 16 17 18 19 20 21 22 23 24

The numbers in red are even. The numbers in blue are odd.

Multiples

These are just the numbers in **multiplication tables**.

For example, multiples of 6 are 6, 12, 18, 24, . . .

The table below shows the multiplication or **times tables** for numbers up to 10. You are expected to know these tables.

X	1	2	3	4	5	6	7	8	9	10
1	1	2	3	4	5	6	7	8	9	10
2	2	4	6	8	10	12	14	16	18	20
3	3	6	9	12	15	18	21	24	27	30
4	4	8	12	16	20	24	28	32	36	40
5	5	10	15	20	25	30	35	40	45	50
6	6	12	18	24	30	36	42	48	54	60
7	7	14	21	28	35	42	49	56	63	70
8	8	16	24	32	40	48	56	64	72	80
9	9	18	27	36	45	54	63	72	81	90
10	10	20	30	40	50	60	70	80	90	100

The multiplication table can also help you with division.

Example

4 × 6 = 24 so   24 ÷ 6 = 4

6 × 4 = 24 and 24 ÷ 4 = 6

 Knowing your multiplication tables is the key to success. Ask someone to test you on your tables to help you learn them.

KEY TERMS

Make sure you understand these terms before moving on!
- place value
- odd numbers
- even numbers
- multiples

QUICK TEST

1. Write down the even numbers between 9 and 21.

2. Write down the multiples of 6 between 20 and 40.

3. Write the number 27 402 in words.

Numbers 2

Factors

Factors are whole numbers that divide exactly into other numbers. For example, factors of 12 are:

1, 2, 3, 4, 6, 12.

Prime numbers

A prime number has only two factors, 1 and itself. Prime numbers up to 20 are:

2, 3, 5, 7, 11, 13, 17, 19.

Note that 1 is not a prime number. Make sure you know the prime numbers up to 20.

Reciprocals

The **reciprocal** of a number $\frac{a}{x}$ is $\frac{x}{a}$.

Example

The reciprocal of $\frac{2}{3}$ is $\frac{3}{2}$.

The reciprocal of 4 is $\frac{1}{4}$, since $4 = \frac{4}{1}$.

Prime factors

These are factors that are prime. Some numbers can be written as the product of their **prime factors**.

Example

The diagram shows the prime factors of 50.
- Divide 50 by its first prime factor 2.
- Divide 25 by its first prime factor 5.
- Keep on going until the final number is prime.

As a product of its prime factors, 50 may be written as:

$2 \times 5 \times 5 = 50$

or $2 \times 5^2 = 50$ in **index** notation (using powers).

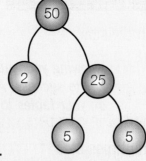

When writing the prime factors of a number, remember to write the final answer as a multiplication.

Highest common factor (HCF)

The **highest factor** that two numbers have in **common** is called the **HCF**.

Example

Find the HCF of 84 and 360.
Write the numbers as products of their prime factors.

$84 = $ ②$ \times $②$ \times $③$ \times 7$
$360 = $②$ \times $②$ \times 2 \times $③$ \times 3 \times 5$

Ring the factors they have in common. These give the HCF $= 2 \times 2 \times 3 = 12$

Lowest common multiple (LCM)

This is the **lowest** number that is a **multiple** of two numbers.

Example

Find the LCM of 6 and 8.
$8 = 2 \times 2 \times 2$
$6 = 2 \times 3$
8 and 6 have a common prime factor of 2, this is only counted once.
LCM of 6 and 8 is $2 \times 2 \times 2 \times 3 = 24$.

Index notation

- An **index** is sometimes known as a **power**.
  6^4 is read as **6 to the power 4**.
  It means $6 \times 6 \times 6 \times 6$.
  5^6 is read as **5 to the power 6**.
  It means $5 \times 5 \times 5 \times 5 \times 5 \times 5$.

  known as the base —— a^b —— known as the index or power

- The base is the value that has to be multiplied. The index indicates how many times.

Powers on a calculator display

The value 5×10^6 means:
$5 \times 10 \times 10 \times 10 \times 10 \times 10 \times 10$
$\qquad = 5\,000\,000$.
On a calculator display 5×10^6 would look like $\boxed{5 \quad ^{06}}$.
On a calculator display 7×10^{19} would look like $\boxed{7 \quad ^{19}}$.

Squares and cubes

- Any number raised to the power 2 gives a **square** number. **For example,** $3^2 = 3 \times 3 = 9$
- Any number raised to the power 3 gives a **cube** number. **For example,** $4^3 = 4 \times 4 \times 4 = 64$

Square numbers include:

   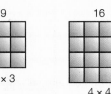

1
1×1

4
2×2

9
3×3

16
4×4

Cube numbers include:

  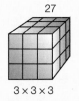

1
$1 \times 1 \times 1$

8
$2 \times 2 \times 2$

27
$3 \times 3 \times 3$

 Square and cube numbers can be represented by diagrams.

Square roots and cube roots

$\sqrt{}$ is the square root sign. Taking the square root is the opposite of squaring, for example, $\sqrt{36} = \pm 6$ since $6 \times 6 = 36$ and $-6 \times -6 = 36$.
$\sqrt[3]{}$ is the cube root sign. Taking the cube root is the opposite of cubing, for example, $\sqrt[3]{64} = 4$ since $4 \times 4 \times 4 = 64$.

KEY TERMS

Make sure you understand these terms before moving on!

- factor
- reciprocal
- prime factors
- index
- power
- square
- cube

QUICK TEST

1. 1 2 3 4 5 6 7 8 9 10 11 12
   From the above numbers write down:
   a any multiples of 3
   b any prime numbers
   c factors of 20
   d even numbers
   e numbers divisible by 5

2. Work these out without a calculator.
   a $\sqrt{100}$
   b 8^2
   c $\sqrt{64}$
   d 2^3.

3. Find the HCF and LCM of 20 and 25.

Positive & negative numbers

Directed numbers

- These are numbers that may be positive or negative.
  Positive are above zero, **negative** are below zero.

  Negative numbers   Positive numbers

  –8 –7 –6 –5 –4 –3 – 2 –1 0 1 2 3 4 5 6 7 8
- Negative numbers are commonly used to describe
  temperatures, i.e. –5°C means 5°C below zero.

Examples –4 is smaller than 4   –2 is bigger than –5

Example Arrange these temperatures in order of size,
smallest first: –6°C, 4°C, –10°C, 3°C, 2°C, –1°C
Arranged in order: –10°C, –6°C, –1°C, 2°C, 3°C, 4°C

If you find working with directed numbers difficult, sketch a quick number line to help you. Remember the rules of multiplication and division; use these laws when multiplying out brackets in algebra.

Negative numbers on the calculator

The [+/–] or [(–)] key on the calculator gives
a negative number.
For example, depending on your make of
calculator: to get –2,
press [2] [+/–] or [(–)] [2]

This represents the sign.

Example
–6 – (–3) = –3
may be keyed in the calculator like this:
[6] [+/–] [–] [3] [+/–] [=]
      sign operation sign

Make sure you know how to enter it in your calculator.

Multiplying and dividing directed numbers

- Multiply and divide the numbers as normal.
- Find the sign for the answer using these rules:

  two like signs (both + or both –) give positive
  two unlike signs (one + and the other –) give negative

$(+) \times (+) = +$
$(-) \times (-) = +$
$(+) \times (-) = -$
$(-) \times (+) = -$
$(+) \div (+) = +$
$(-) \div (-) = +$
$(+) \div (-) = -$
$(-) \div (+) = -$

Examples
–6 × (+4) = –24   –3 × (–4) = 12   –24 ÷ (–2) = 12   15 ÷ (–3) = –5

Multiply or divide as normal, then put in the sign.

Adding and subtracting directed numbers

- When adding and subtracting directed numbers it is helpful to draw a number line.

Example

The temperature at 3 pm was 2°C; by 11 pm it had dropped
by 7 degrees. What was the temperature at 11 pm?

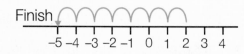

The temperature at 11 pm was –5°C.

Example

Find the value of –2 – 7 (note the different uses of the minus sign).

$$-2 - 7$$

This represents the sign of
the number, so start at –2.

This represents the operation
of subtraction, so move
7 places to the left.

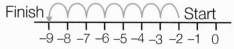

- When the number to be added (or subtracted) is negative, the normal direction of
movement is reversed.

Example

$$-6 - (-1) \text{ is the same as } -6 + 1 = -5.$$

The negative changes the direction.   Move 1 place to the right.

- When two (+) signs or two (–) signs are together then use these rules:

+(+) = + ⎫ **Like** signs give
–(–) = + ⎬ a **positive**.

+(–) = – ⎫ **Unlike** signs give
–(+) = – ⎬ a **negative**.

Examples

–2 + (–3) = –2 – 3 = –5   –4 – (+4) = –4 – 4 = –8
5 – (–2) = 5 + 2 = 7   6 + (–2) = 6 – 2 = 4

KEY TERMS

Make sure you
understand these
terms before moving on!
- positive numbers
- negative numbers

QUICK TEST

1. The temperature inside the house is
   12 degrees higher than outside.

   If the temperature outside is –5°C, what is
   the temperature inside?

2. Work out what the missing letters stand for.

   a 12 – A = –3   b –6 + 10 = B

   c –9 × C = –36   d –8 – D = 2

   e 120 ÷ E = –12   f 14 + F = –6

Working with numbers

Addition and subtraction

When **adding** and **subtracting** numbers, remember that their place values must line up, one below the other.

Example
4279 + 368

Line up the numbers first.

$$
\begin{array}{r}
4279 \\
368 + \\
\hline
4647 \\
\scriptstyle 1\ 1
\end{array}
$$

The one is carried here into the 10s column.

Add the units, then the 10s and so on.

Example
2791 – 365

$$
\begin{array}{r}
27\overset{8}{9}\overset{1}{1} \\
365 - \\
\hline
2426
\end{array}
$$

Subtract the numbers in the unit column.
1 – 5 won't work. Borrow 10 from the next column. So the 9 becomes an 8 and the 1 becomes 11.

Multiplication and division

Questions on **multiplication** and **division** will be difficult unless you know your times tables.

Example

$$
\begin{array}{r}
274 \\
4 \times \\
\hline
1096 \\
\scriptstyle 2\ 1
\end{array}
$$

Multiply the single-digit number by each digit of the large number.

Start with the units, then the tens and so on.

When the answer is 10 or more carry the tens digit to the next column.

Example

$$
3\,\overline{)1^{1}209}\ =\ 403
$$

Divide 3 into the large number one digit at a time.

Put the result of each division on the top.

Carry the remainder if 3 will not go in exactly.

Long division

A vase costs 74p. Tracey has £9.82 to spend. What is the maximum number of vases Tracey can buy? How much change does she have left? Do this calculation without using a calculator.

$$
\begin{array}{r}
13 \\
74\,\overline{)982} \\
74\ - \\
\hline
242 \\
222\ - \\
\hline
20
\end{array}
$$

Step 1: 74 goes into 98 once, put down 1
Step 2: Subtract 74 from 98
Step 3: Bring down the 2
Step 4: Divide 74 into 242, put down the 3
Step 5: 74 × 3 = 222
Step 6: 242 – 222 = remainder 20

Tracey can buy 13 vases and has 20p left over.

Long multiplication

Example
A single plant costs 42p. Without a calculator work out the cost of 164 plants.

$$
\begin{array}{r}
164 \\
42 \times \\
\hline
328 \\
6560 + \\
\hline
6888
\end{array}
$$

Step 1: 164 × 2
Step 2: 164 × 40
Step 3: 328 + 6560

Cost = 6888p or £68.88.

 Make your working out clear.

Multiplication and division by 10, 100, 1000

To multiply by 10, 100, 1000 etc., move the digits one, two, three, ... , places to the left and put in zeros if necessary.

Examples

15.2 × 10	= 152	Move the digits one place to the left.
53 × 10	= 530	Put in a zero, after moving the digits one place to the left.
15.2 × 100	= 1520	Move the digits two places to the left.
53 × 100	= 5300	Put in two zeros, after moving the digits two places to the left.
15.2 × 1000	= 15 200	Move the digits three places to the left.
53 × 1000	= 53 000	Put in three zeros, after moving the digits three places to the left.

To divide by 10, 100, 1000, ... move the digits one, two, three, ... , places to the right.

Examples

$$15.8 \div 10 = 1.58 \qquad 56 \div 100 = 0.56 \qquad 18.2 \div 1000 = 0.0182$$

When multiplying by multiples of 10 (such as 20, 30, 700) the same rules apply, except you multiply the numbers first then move the digits to the left.

Examples

$$50 \times 30 = 50 \times 3 \times 10 = 150 \times 10 = 1500$$
$$2.4 \times 20 = 2.4 \times 2 \times 10 = 4.8 \times 10 = 48$$

When dividing by multiples of 10, the same rules apply, except you divide the numbers and then move the digits to the right.

Examples

$$6000 \div 20 = 6000 \div 2 \div 10 = 3000 \div 10 = 300$$
$$9.3 \div 30 = 9.3 \div 3 \div 10 = 3.1 \div 10 = 0.31$$

Try to master all the different methods on these pages as they are likely to be tested on the non-calculator paper and possibly the mental arithmetic paper too!

QUICK TEST

Answer the following questions.

1. a 279
       426 +

    b 639
       148 −

    c 276
         8 ×

    d 5)‾1275‾

2. 279
     47 ×

3. 37)‾925‾

4. Without a calculator work out the following.

    a 15.2 × 10   b 6.3 × 100   c 21 × 1000   d 25.2 ÷ 100

5. A tin of soup costs 68p. Without using a calculator, work out the cost of 18 tins.

6. The cost of a trip is £10.25. If Mr Appleyard collects in £133.25 how many people are going on the trip? Work this out without using a calculator.

Fractions

- A fraction is part of a whole one. $\frac{2}{5}$ means 2 parts out of 5.

- The top number is the *numerator*, the bottom one is the *denominator*.

- A fraction like $\frac{2}{5}$ is called a *proper fraction*.

- A fraction like $\frac{12}{7}$ is called an *improper fraction*.

- A fraction like $1\frac{4}{9}$ is called a *mixed number*.

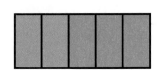

Addition and subtraction of fractions

The example shows the basic principles of adding and subtracting fractions.

Example

$\frac{1}{8} + \frac{3}{4}$ First make the denominators the same. $\frac{3}{4} = \frac{6}{8}$

$\frac{1}{8} + \frac{6}{8}$ Replace $\frac{3}{4}$ with $\frac{6}{8}$ so that the denominators are now the same.

$= \frac{7}{8}$ Add the numerators. $1 + 6 = 7$
Do not add the denominators.
The denominator stays the same.

Example

$\frac{3}{4} - \frac{3}{16}$ First make the denominators the same. $\frac{3}{4} = \frac{12}{16}$

$\frac{3}{4}$ is equivalent to $\frac{12}{16}$.

$\frac{3}{16} - \frac{3}{16}$ Replace $\frac{3}{4}$ with $\frac{12}{16}$.

Subtract the numerators but not the denominators.
The denominator stays the same.

$= \frac{9}{16}$

Proportional changes with fractions

Fractions of a quantity
The word of means multiply.

Example In a class of 40 students, $\frac{2}{5}$ of them are left-handed.
How many are left-handed?

$\frac{2}{5}$ of 40 means $\frac{2}{5} \times 40 = 16$ students

On the calculator key in: $\boxed{2}\ \boxed{\div}\ \boxed{5}\ \boxed{\times}\ \boxed{4}\ \boxed{0}\ \boxed{=}$

Alternatively, divide 40 by 5 to find $\frac{1}{5}$ then

multiply by 2 to find $\frac{2}{5}$.

KEY TERMS

Make sure you understand these terms before moving on!
- numerator
- denominator
- proper fraction
- improper fraction
- mixed number

Multiplication and division of fractions

When multiplying and dividing fractions, write out whole or mixed numbers as improper fractions.

For example rewrite $2\frac{1}{2}$ as $\frac{5}{2}$.

Example

$$\frac{4}{7} \times \frac{2}{11} = \frac{8}{77}$$

Multiply the numerators together.
Multiply the denominators together.

For division, change it into a multiplication by turning the second fraction upside down (taking the reciprocal) and multiply both fractions together.

Example

$$\frac{7}{9} \div \frac{12}{18}$$

Turn $\frac{12}{18}$ upside down and multiply with $\frac{7}{9}$.

$$\frac{7}{9} \times \frac{18}{12} = \frac{126}{108} = 1\frac{1}{6}$$

Give the answer as a mixed number.

The fraction key

$\boxed{a^b/c}$ is the fraction key on the calculator.

Example

$\frac{20}{30}$ is keyed in as $\boxed{2}\,\boxed{0}\,\boxed{a^b/c}\,\boxed{3}\,\boxed{0}$

This is displayed as

$\boxed{20\ \ulcorner\ 30}$ or $\boxed{20\ \lrcorner\ 30}$

The calculator will automatically cancel fractions when the $\boxed{=}$ key is pressed. For example, $\frac{20}{30}$ becomes $\boxed{2\lrcorner 3}$ or $\boxed{2\ulcorner 3}$.

This means two-thirds

A display of $\boxed{1\lrcorner 5\lrcorner 7}$ means $1\frac{5}{7}$.

If you now press $\boxed{\text{shift}}\,\boxed{a^b/c}$, it converts to an improper fraction $\frac{12}{7}$.

Check: your calculator may have a $\boxed{\text{2nd}}\,\boxed{\text{inv}}$ instead of $\boxed{\text{shift}}$.

Equivalent fractions

■ These are fractions that have the same value.

Example

From the diagram it can be seen that $\frac{1}{2} = \frac{2}{4}$.

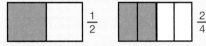

■ Fractions can be changed into an equivalent by either multiplying or dividing the numerator and denominator by the same number.

Examples

$\frac{7}{9} = \frac{?}{27}$

$\overset{\times 3}{\frac{7}{9} = \frac{21}{27}}$
$\underset{\times 3}{}$

Multiply the top and bottom by 3.

$\frac{35}{50} = \frac{7}{?}$

$\overset{\div 5}{\frac{35}{50} = \frac{7}{10}}$
$\underset{\div 5}{}$

Divide the top and bottom by 5.

Simplifying fractions

Fractions can be simplified if the numerator and the denominator have a common factor.

Example

Simplify $\frac{12}{18}$.

6 is the highest common factor of 12 and 18. Divide both the top and bottom number by 6. So $\frac{12}{18}$ is simplified to $\frac{2}{3}$.

1. Work out the missing values.
   a $\frac{7}{12} = \frac{14}{x}$ b $\frac{125}{500} = \frac{y}{100}$ c $\frac{19}{38} = \frac{76}{z}$

2. Work out the following.
   a $\frac{2}{9} + \frac{3}{27}$ b $\frac{3}{5} - \frac{1}{4}$ c $\frac{6}{9} \times \frac{72}{104}$ d $\frac{8}{9} \div \frac{2}{3}$

3. $\frac{5}{8}$ of a class of 24 walk to school. How many pupils walk to school?

Questions involving fractions are quite common on the non-calculator paper. Learn the quick way of finding a fraction of a quantity.

Decimals

What are decimals?

- The number of digits after the decimal point tells us how many decimal places there are. For example 6.786 has three decimal places, there are 3 numbers after the decimal point.
- The **decimal point** separates whole-number columns from fractional columns.

Thousands	Hundreds	Tens	Units	•	Tenths	Hundredths	Thousandths
6	7	1	4	•	2	3	8

Decimal point

- The 2 means $\frac{2}{10}$.   • The 3 means $\frac{3}{100}$.   • The 8 means $\frac{8}{1000}$.

Recurring decimals

- A number or group of numbers that **recurs** in a decimal is shown by placing a dot over the first and last numbers that repeat.

Example

$$0.66666 \ldots = 0.\dot{6} \qquad\qquad 0.147147 \ldots = 0.\dot{1}4\dot{7}$$

 Remember, hundredths are smaller than tenths, $\frac{3}{100}$ is smaller than $\frac{2}{10}$.

Multiplying and dividing decimals by 10, 100 and 1000

To **multiply** a **decimal** number by 10, move the digits one place to the **left**.   **Example** $3.7 \times 10 = 37$

A similar rule can be used when multiplying decimal numbers by 100 and 1000.

- To multiply a decimal number by 100, move the digits two places to the left.   **Example** $11.42 \times 100 = 1142$
- To multiply a decimal number by 1000, move the digits three places to the left and put in zeros if necessary.
  Example $231.4 \times 1000 = 231\,400$

Multiply by 10

Hundreds	Tens	Units	•	Tenths	Hundredths	Thousandths
		3	•	7		
	3	7	•			

When **dividing** decimal numbers by 10, move the digits one place to the **right**.   **Example** $48.2 \div 10 = 4.82$

- When dividing a decimal number by 100, move the digits two places to the right.   **Example** $127.3 \div 100 = 1.273$
- When dividing a decimal number by 1000, move the digits three places to the right.
  Example $15.62 \div 1000 = 0.01562$

Divide by 10

Hundreds	Tens	Units	•	Tenths	Hundredths	Thousandths
	4	8	•	2		
		4	•	8	2	

Decimals are frequently used when dealing with money. When changing pounds to pence multiply the decimal by 100, and when changing pence to pounds divide the number by 100.

Calculations with decimals

Calculations with decimals are similar to calculations with whole numbers.

Examples

1 Add together 6.21 and 4.9.

$$6.21$$
$$+ 4.90$$
$$\overline{11.11}$$

Put the decimal points under each other.

This is the same as 4.9. The decimal points in the answer will be in line.

2 Subtract 6.2 from 12.81.

$$12.81$$
$$6.20 -$$
$$\overline{6.61}$$

> *When adding or subtracting decimals make sure they have the same number of places, 4.9 = 4.90.*

3 Multiply 12.3 by 7.

$$12.3$$
$$7 \times$$
$$\overline{861}$$

Answer = 86.1

Multiply 123 by 7 = 861, ignoring the decimal point. Since 12.3 has one number after the decimal point then so must the answer.

4 Divide 25.8 by 6.

$$\begin{array}{r} 4.3 \\ 6\overline{\smash{)}25.8} \end{array}$$

Divide as normal, keeping the decimal points in line.

Ordering decimals

When ordering decimals:
- first write them with the same number of figures after the decimal point
- then compare whole numbers, digits in the tenths place, digits in the hundredths place, and so on.

Example

Arrange these numbers in order of size, smallest first. 4.27, 4.041, 4.7, 6.4, 2.19, 4.72
First rewrite them: 4.270, 4.041, 4.700, 6.400, 2.190, 4.720
Then reorder them: 2.190   4.041   4.270   4.700   4.720   6.400

> *Have a quick check that all values are included.*   Zero is smaller than 2.

KEY TERMS

Make sure you understand these terms before moving on!
- decimal point
- recurring decimal
- decimal

QUICK TEST

Work out the answers to the following questions.

1 a 27.9
        143.07 +

   b 16.05
      12.21 −

   c 27.8
        3 ×

   d $4\overline{\smash{)}62.8}$

2 a 14.6 × 10   b 12.57 × 100   c 3.21 × 1000
     d 9.7 ÷ 10   e 271 ÷ 100   f 26 ÷ 1000

3 Arrange these numbers in order of size, smallest first.
     a 0.62, 0.03, 0.84, 0.037
     b 27.06, 22.53, 22.507, 27.064

Percentages

- Percentages are fractions with a denominator of 100.
- % is the percentage sign.
- 75% means $\frac{75}{100}$ (this is equal to $\frac{3}{4}$).

Percentages of a quantity

Replace the word 'of' with a × sign.
Rewrite the **percentage** as a fraction.

Example
Find 15% of £650.

$\frac{15}{100}$ × 650 = £97.50

On the calculator key in

| 1 | 5 | ÷ | 1 | 0 | 0 | × | 6 | 5 | 0 | = |

- To work it out mentally, find
  10% = 650 ÷ 10 = £65
  5% is half of £65 = £32.50
  Add the two together to give £97.50.

Example
Work out $17\frac{1}{2}$% of 360 without using a calculator.

$$10\% \text{ of } 360 = 36$$
$$5\% \text{ of } 360 = 18$$
$$2\frac{1}{2}\% \text{ of } 360 = 9$$

So $17\frac{1}{2}$% of 360 = 36 + 18 + 9
= 63

Percentage questions appear frequently at KS3. If there is a percentage question on the non-calculator paper, work out what 10% is equal to as shown in the examples.

One quantity as a percentage of another

Rule: To make the answer a percentage, multiply by 100%.

Make a fraction with the two numbers.
Multiply by 100% to get a percentage.

Example
A survey shows that 26 people out of 45 preferred 'Supersuds' washing powder.
What percentage preferred Supersuds?

$\frac{26}{45}$ × 100% = 57.$\dot{7}$% = 57.8% (1 dp)

On the calculator key in | 2 | 6 | ÷ | 4 | 5 | × | 1 | 0 | 0 | = |

Example
In a carton of milk, 6.2 g of the contents are fat.
If 2.5 g of the fat is saturated what percentage is this?

Make the fraction.

$\frac{2.5}{6.2}$ × 100% = 40.3% (1 dp)

× by 100%

Increasing and decreasing by a percentage

Percentages will often appear in real-life problems.
You will often need to find the new value when the amount has been increased or decreased by a percentage.

Example

A new car was bought for £8600. After 2 years, it had lost 30% of its value.
Work out the value of the car after 2 years. Use a non-calculator method.

100% = £8600

10% = 8600 ÷ 10
    = £860

30% = 860 × 3
    = £2580

This can be calculated by multiplying by $1 + \frac{27}{100} = 1.27$.
This is known as the **multiplier**.

Value of car after 2 years = original − decrease
                          = 8600 − 2580
                          = £6020

Example

In 1998 the average price of a 3 bedroomed house was £72 000.
In 2001, the average price of a 3 bedroomed house had risen by 27%.
Work out the average price in 2001.

100% = £72 000
Increase = 27% of £72 000

        = $\frac{27}{100}$ × 72 000 = £19 440

Average price of house in 2001 = £72 000 + £19 440
                              = £91 440

To find 10% remember to divide (÷) by 10.
Remember, 'of' means multiply (×).
Remember to answer the whole question!

KEY TERMS

Make sure you understand these terms before moving on!
- percentage
- multiplier

❶ Of 30 people at a bus stop, 10% wear glasses. How many people at the bus stop wear glasses?

❷ 25% of the students in year 9 choose Maths as their favourite subject. If there are 140 students in the year, how many choose Maths?

❸ If 20% of a number is 8 what is the number?

❹ There are 62 cars in a car park: 14 are white. What percentage are white? Ⓒ

❺ The top mark in a Maths test was 59 out of 72. Write this as a percentage. Ⓒ

❻ A jumper costs £60. If the price is reduced by 15% in a sale how much does it now cost?

❼ The number of people who go swimming in the morning is 30. If this rises by 20%, how many now go swimming in the morning?

Equivalents

Useful equivalents

Fractions, **decimals** and **percentages** all mean the same thing but are just written in a different way.

The table shows some common fractions and their **equivalents** which you need to learn. You need to know how to convert:

to → to
fractions → decimals → percentages.

Fraction	Decimal	Percentage
$\frac{1}{2}$ ($1 \div 2$)	0.5 ($\times 100\%$)	50%
$\frac{1}{3}$	$0.\dot{3}$	$33.\dot{3}\%$
$\frac{2}{3}$	$0.\dot{6}$	$66.\dot{6}\%$
$\frac{1}{4}$	0.25	25%
$\frac{3}{4}$	0.75	75%
$\frac{1}{5}$	0.2	20%
$\frac{1}{8}$	0.125	12.5%
$\frac{3}{8}$	0.375	37.5%
$\frac{1}{10}$	0.1	10%
$\frac{1}{100}$	0.01	1%

Ordering different numbers

When putting fractions, decimals and percentages in **order** of size, it is best to change them all to decimals first.

Example Place in order of size, smallest first.

$\frac{1}{4}$, 0.241, 29%, 64%, $\frac{1}{3}$

0.25, 0.241, 0.29, 0.64, $0.\dot{3}$ Put into decimals first.
0.241, 0.25, 0.29, $0.\dot{3}$, 0.64   Now order.
0.241, $\frac{1}{4}$, 29%, $\frac{1}{3}$, 64%   Now rewrite in the original form.

> 💡 *Make sure you put the values in the order the question says. Ask a friend to test you on equivalent fractions, decimals and percentages because you need to learn them.*

❶ Complete the table.

Fraction (simplest form)	Decimal	Percentage
		75%
$\frac{2}{5}$		
	$0.\dot{3}$	
	0.6	
		20%

❷ Arrange these numbers in order of size, smallest first.
$\frac{2}{3}$, 0.25, $\frac{5}{9}$, 84%, $\frac{9}{10}$.

QUICK TEST

KEY TERMS
Make sure you understand these terms before moving on!
- fractions
- decimals
- percentage
- equivalents
- order
- BIDMAS

Using a calculator

Order of operations

BIDMAS is a made up word which helps you to remember the order in which to make calculations.

$$B \quad I \quad D \quad M \quad A \quad S$$

Brackets Indices or Powers Division Multiplication Addition Subtraction

This just means that brackets are carried out first, then the others are done in order.

Examples $(2 + 4) \times 3 = 18$ $6 + 2 \times 4 = 14$ ←——— Not 32 because multiplication is done first.

Interpreting the calculator display

When questions involve money remember the following points:

- a display of 6.7 means £6.70 (six pounds seventy pence).
- a display of 5.03 means £5.03 (five pounds three pence).

- a display of 0.82 means £0.82 or 82 pence.
- a display of 6.2934 needs to be rounded to 2 dp to give £6.29.
- a display of $4.^{07}$ means 4×10^7.

Important calculator keys

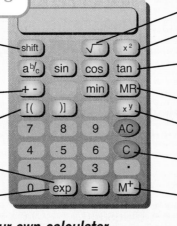

shift or 2nd or Inv allows 2nd functions to be carried out.

− or +/− changes positive numbers to negative ones.

bracket keys

often puts the ×10 part in when working in standard form.

pressing shift EXP often gives π

square root
square button
trigonometric buttons
memory keys
works out powers
cancels only the last key you have pressed
memory keys

💡 *It is very important that you can use your own calculator. Practise questions with a friend so that you become confident.*

QUICK TEST

1. Work these out without a calculator. a $3 + 2 \times 4$ b $(6 + 2) \times 3$ c $27 \div 3 + 2$

2. Work these out on your calculator.   a $3^2 + \sqrt{25}$ b $\dfrac{6 + 2}{4}$ c $5 + 3 \times 6$
   Now check these answers mentally.

3. Jonathan's calculator display shows $1.52^{\ 06}$. Write down what the display means.

Rounding

Rounding numbers to the nearest ten, hundred, thousand

Large numbers are often **approximated** to the nearest ten, hundred, thousand and so on.

Rounding to the nearest ten
Look at the digit in the units column. If it is less than 5, round down. If it is 5 or more, round up.

27 000 attend opening of Theme Park
26 842 people attended the

Example
Round 568 to the nearest ten.
There is an 8 in the units column, so round up to 570.
568 is 570 to the nearest ten.

 568 is closer to 570 than 560.

Rounding to the nearest hundred
Look at the digit in the tens column. If it is less than 5, round down. If it is 5 or more, round up.

Example
Round 2650 to the nearest hundred.
There is a 5 in the tens column, so round up to 2700.
2650 is 2700 to the nearest hundred.

Rounding to the nearest thousand
Look at the digit in the hundreds column. The same rules apply as before.

Example
Round 16 420 to the nearest thousand.
There is a 4 in the hundreds column, so round down to 16 000.
16 420 is 16 000 to the nearest thousand.

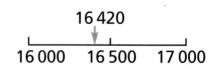

 Sketch a number line if it helps.

Decimal places (dp)

To round to a specified number of **decimal places**:
- look at the last digit that is wanted (if rounding 8.347 to 2 d.p. look at the 4 – second decimal place)
- look at the number after it (look at the number not needed, i.e. the 7)
- if it is **5 or more** round up the last digit (7 is greater than 5, so round the 4 up to a 5)
- if it is **less than 5**, the digit remains the same
- so to 2dp 8.347 = 8.35.

Example
Ruby runs the 100m in 14.87 seconds.
What is her time to 1 decimal place?

14.8<u>7</u>   14.9

Since this number is greater than 5
we round the 8 up to a 9.

Example
Samuel has the number 274.7325 on his calculator display.
Round this number to 3 decimal places.

274.732<u>5</u> (4dp)   274.733 (3dp)

Since this number is 5 we
round the 2 up to a 3.

Examples
16.5<u>9</u> = 16.6 to 1 dp.
8.43<u>5</u> = 8.44 to 2 dp.
12.3<u>4</u> = 12.3 to 1 dp.
274.63<u>8</u> = 274.64 to 2 dp.
29.378<u>5</u> = 29.379 to 3 dp.
9.62<u>79</u> = 9.63 to 2 dp.
736.2<u>984</u> = 736.3 to 1 dp.

When you are asked to round to a number of decimal places, check that you do not move the decimal point and that the correct number of digits are after the decimal point.

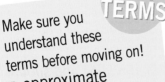

KEY TERMS

Make sure you understand these terms before moving on!
- approximate
- rounding
- decimal place

QUICK TEST

1. Round 6.493 to 2 decimal places.
2. Round 12.059 to 2 decimal places.
3. Round 9.47 to 1 decimal place.
4. Round 1247 to the nearest 100.
5. Round 1379 to the nearest 1000.
6. Round the following to the nearest 10.
   a 265   b 7293   c 1469   d 25352

Estimates & checking calculation

Checking calculations

When you are checking calculations, you can reverse the process like this.

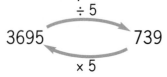

3695   ÷ 5   739
    × 5

Example

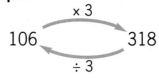

106   × 3   318
   ÷ 3

$106 \times 3 = 318$
Check: $318 \div 3 = 106$

Estimates and approximations

Estimating is a good way of checking answers.
- Round the numbers to 'easy' numbers, usually to the nearest 10, 100 or 1000.
- Use these easy numbers to work out the estimate.
- Use the symbol ≈, which means '**approximately equal to**'.

When multiplying or dividing, never approximate a number with zero.
Use 0.1, 0.01, 0.001, … .

Examples
a $12 \times 406 \approx 10 \times 400 = 4000$
b $(6.29)^2 \approx 6^2 = 36$
c $\frac{296 \times 52.1}{9.72 \times 1.14} \approx \frac{300 \times 50}{10 \times 1} = \frac{15\,000}{10} = 1500$
d $0.096 \times 79.2 \approx 0.1 \times 80 = 8$

> *Questions that involve approximating are likely to be on the non-calculator paper. Remember to approximate to the nearest 10, 100 or 1000.*

Example

Q   Jack does the calculation $\frac{9.6 \times 103}{2.9^2}$.

   a **Estimate** the answer to this calculation, without using a calculator.
   b Jack's answer is 1175.7. Is this the right order of magnitude?

> *Right order of magnitude means 'about the right size'.*

A   a Estimate $\frac{9.6 \times 103}{2.9^2} \approx \frac{10 \times 100}{3^2} = \frac{1000}{9} \approx \frac{1000}{10} = 100$

   b Jack's answer is not the right order of magnitude. It is 10 times too big.

Examples
a $109.6 + 0.0002 \approx 110 + 0 = 110$
b $63.87 - 0.01 \approx 64 - 0 = 64$

> *When adding and subtracting, very small numbers may be approximated to zero.*

Calculations

When you are solving problems your answers should be rounded sensibly.

Example
Cans of drink come in packs of 6.

Q a How many 6-packs are needed for 33 people?

b How many are left over?

A a $33 \div 6 = 5$ remainder 3, so 6 packs of drink are needed.

b $6 \times 6 = 36$ cans of drink, so 3 cans will be left over.

Example
$95.26 \times 6.39 = 608.7114 = 608.71$ (2 dp)

 Round to 2 dp because the values in the question are given to 2 dp.

Example
Jackie has £9.37. She divides it equally among 5 people. How much does each person receive?

$£9.37 \div 5 = £1.874$

$\qquad\qquad = £1.87$

 Round to 1.87 as it is money.

When rounding remainders, consider the context of the question.

Example
Paint is sold in 8-litre tins. Sandra needs 27 litres of paint. How many tins must she buy?

$27 \div 8 = 3$ remainder 3

Sandra needs four tins of paint.

Sandra would not have enough paint with three tins, since she would be three litres short. Hence the number of tins of paint must be rounded up.

QUICK TEST

Estimate the answers to the following questions.

① a $41 + 69$ b $299 \div 29$ c $3.1^2 + 29 \times 31$

② Sukhvinder decided to decorate her living room. The total area of the walls was $48\,m^2$. If one roll of wallpaper covers $5\,m^2$ of wall, how many rolls of wallpaper will Sukvhinder need? **ⓒ**

③ Mr Singh organised a trip to the theatre. 420 students and 10 teachers were going on the trip. If a coach can seat 53 people, how many coaches did he need? **ⓒ**

④ Thomas earned £109.25 for working a 23-hour week. How much did he earn per hour? Estimate, then use a calculator. **ⓒ**

Ratio

What is a ratio?

A **ratio** is used to compare two or more quantities. '**Compared to**' is replaced with **two dots**(:). **For example,** '16 boys compared to 20 girls' can be written as 16 : 20. To simplify ratios, divide both parts of the ratio by the highest common factor.

For example, 16 : 20 = 4 : 5 (divide both parts by 4).

Examples

Simplify the ratio 21:28.
21:28 = 3:4 Divide both parts by 7.
The ratio of yellow flowers to blue flowers can be written as:

$$10 : 4 = \frac{10}{2} : \frac{4}{2}$$
$$= 5 : 2$$

In other words, for every 5 yellow flowers there are 2 blue flowers.

To express the ratio 5 : 2 as the ratio $n : 1$ divide both sides by 2.

$$\frac{5}{2} : \frac{2}{2} = 2.5 : 1$$

Best buys

Compare **unit amounts** to decide which is the better value for money.

Example

The same brand of breakfast cereal is sold in packets of two different sizes. Which packet represents the better value for money?

- Find the cost per gram for each packet.
  125 g = £1.06   Cost of 1 g = 106 ÷ 125 = 0.848p.
  750 g = £2.81   Cost of 1 g = 281 ÷ 750 = 0.3746p.
- Since the 750 g packet costs less per gram, it is better value for money.

BREKKO FLAKES
750 g
£2.81

BREKKO FLAKES
125g
£1.06

Sharing a quantity in a given ratio

- Add up the total parts.
- Work out what one part is worth.
- Work out what the other parts are worth.

Example

A forest covers 25 000 hectares. Oak and ash trees are planted in the forest in the ratio 2 : 3. How many hectares do the ash trees cover?

- 2 + 3 = 5 parts
- 5 parts = 25 000 hectares
- 1 part = $\frac{25\,000}{5}$ = 5000 hectares

Ash has 3 parts, i.e. 3 × 5000
= 15 000 hectares.

 A quick check is to work out the number of hectares the oak trees cover. The total of the oak + ash should be equal to 25 000 hectares.

Increasing and decreasing in a given ratio

- Divide to get one part.
- Multiply for each new part.

 When answering problems that involve ratios, always try to work out what a unit (or one) is worth. You should then be able to work out what any other value is worth.

Example

A photograph of length 9 cm is to be enlarged in the ratio 5 : 3. What is the length of the enlarged photograph?
- Divide 9 cm by 3 to get one part. $9 \div 3 = 3$ cm for one part.
- Multiply this by 5. So $5 \times 3 = 15$ cm on the enlarged photograph.

Example

Eight people took 6 days to build a house.
At the same rate how long would it take 3 people?
- Time for 8 people = 6 days.
- Time for 1 person = $8 \times 6 = 48$ days.
It takes one person longer to build the house.
- Time for 3 people = $\frac{48}{3} = 16$ days.

Three people will take $\frac{1}{3}$ of the time taken by 1 person.

Example

A recipe for 4 people needs 1600g of flour.
How much flour is needed for the same recipe for 6 people?
- Divide 1600g by 4, so 400g for 1 person.
- Multiply by 6, so $6 \times 400g = 2400g$ for 6 people.

FLOUR

Example

A photocopier is set to reduce in the ratio of 3 : 5. What is the length of the reduced diagram if the original length is 12 cm?
- Divide 12 by 5 to get 1 part = 2.4 cm.
- Multiply this by 3 to get $3 \times 2.4 = 7.2$ cm.

QUICK TEST

1. Write the following ratios in their simplest form.
   a 12 : 15   b 6 : 12   c 25 : 10

2. Ahmed and Fiona share £500 between them in the ratio 2 : 3. How much does each receive?

3. A recipe for 12 people uses 500g of plain flour. How much flour is needed for 18 people?

4. If 15 oranges cost £1.80, how much will 23 identical oranges cost? **c**

5. The same brand of tuna fish is sold in tins of two different sizes. Which tin represents the better value for money? **c**

 48p
TUNA
198 g

 76p
TUNA
240 g

KEY TERMS

...ke sure you ...derstand these ...ms before moving on!

ratio
unit amount

Practice questions

Use the questions to test your progress. Check your answers on page 87.

1. Use digits to write these numbers.

   a ninety-two .... **b** four hundred and seven .... **c** three thousand and sixty ....

2. What is the place value of the 7 in each of these?

   a 47 .... **b** 76 .... **c** 4971 .... **d** 7369 ....

3. Write the number 3 248 020 in words.

   ....

4. Put these numbers in order, smallest to biggest.

   a 379   428   27   6394   6492   787   ....

   b 793   487   478   496   527   1348   12   ....

5. This is a multiplication square.
   Fill in the missing numbers.

×	2	9	4
6			
3			
5			

6. Work out the following without using a calculator.

   a   6214
      298 +
     ....

   b   6351
     2170 −
     ....

   c   3259
       7 ×
     ....

   d ....
     6 ⟌ 1290

7. The temperature inside the house is 20 degrees higher than outside.
   If the temperature outside is −5°C, what is the temperature inside?

   ....

8. Round these numbers to the nearest 10.

   a 62 .... **b** 55 .... **c** 128 ....

   Round these numbers to the nearest 100.

   d 146 .... **e** 289 .... **f** 1350 ....

   Round these numbers to the nearest 1000.

   g 7449 .... **h** 8826 ....

9.   1   2   3   4
       5   6   7   8
       9 10 11 12

   From the above numbers write down all the:

   a multiples of 4 ....

   b prime numbers ....

   c factors of 12 ....

10. Write 24 as a product of prime factors. ....

11. Work these out without using a calculator.

   a $\sqrt{100}$ .... **b** 6^2 .... **c** $\sqrt{36}$ .... **d** 2^3 ....

12. Jonathan's calculator display shows $\boxed{2.76^{\ 09}}$. Write down what the calculator display means.

   ....

13. Work out the missing values. (C)

   a $\dfrac{7}{12} = \dfrac{14}{\ }$ .... **b** $\dfrac{125}{500} = \dfrac{y}{100}$ .... **c** $\dfrac{19}{38} = \dfrac{76}{\ }$ ....

14. On a flag, 27% is coloured red, 61% is blue and the rest is yellow. What percentage is yellow?

   ....

15. If an apple costs 18p, work out the cost of 78 similar apples.

   ....

16. Jessica buys some tins of cat food at a total cost of £8.46. If each tin costs 47p, how many tins does Jessica buy?

   ....

17. Work out the number represented by each letter.

   a $11 + A = 6$ .... **b** $-8 + 7 = B$ .... **c** $-9 - C = 3$ .... **d** $10 - D = 3$ ....

18. A jumper costs £45. In a sale its price is reduced by 15%; how much does it now cost?

   ....

19. An orchard is planted with 1600 apple and plum trees in the ratio 3 : 5. How many apple trees are in the orchard?

   ....

20. A map is being enlarged in the ratio 12 : 7. If the original road length was 21 cm on the map, what is the length of the road on the enlarged map?

   ....

21. Work out the following. **a** $\dfrac{2}{5} + \dfrac{3}{10}$ .... **b** $\dfrac{2}{3} - \dfrac{1}{2}$ .... **c** $\dfrac{3}{10} \times \dfrac{5}{8}$ ....

22. Round the following to two decimal places.

   a 12.693 .... **b** 28.756 .... **c** 2.935 ....

23. Complete the table.

Fraction	Decimal	Percentage
....	....	25%
$\dfrac{5}{8}$	....	....
....	$0.\dot{6}$	....

24. Place these values in order, putting the smallest first. 61% 94% 0.93 $\dfrac{9}{10}$ $\dfrac{4}{7}$ 0.274

   ....

(C) A calculator may be used.

Algebra 1

Algebraic conventions

- **Algebra** uses letters to represent numbers.
- A **term** is made up of numbers and letters multiplied together.
- An **expression** is made up of terms that are connected by +, − and may include brackets.

$$3xy - 5r + 2x^2 - 4$$

invisible + sign xy term r term x^2 term   number term

Follow these rules when writing algebra.

$$a + a + a + a = 4a$$
$$b \times b = b^2 \quad \textbf{not } 2b$$
$$b \times b \times b = b^3 \quad \textbf{not } 3b$$
$$n \times n \times 3 = 3n^2 \quad \textbf{not } (3n)^2$$
$$a \times 3 \times c = 3ac$$

💡 *Put the number first and then the letters in alphabetical order; leave out the multiplication signs.*

- Division such as $a \div 3$, is usually written as a fraction, $\frac{a}{3}$.

Using letters

Example

Emily plants a small vegetable garden with potatoes, carrots and onions. m stands for the number of carrot seeds she sows. If she sows five more onion seeds than carrot seeds, how many onion seeds does she sow?

$$m + 5 \qquad \text{This is an \textbf{expression}.}$$

If she sows half as many onion seeds as carrot seeds, this is $m \div 2$ which is usually written as $\frac{m}{2}$.

💡 *Remember, in algebra a division is usually written as a fraction $x \div a = \frac{x}{a}$.*

Example

Richard has p counters. David has three times as many counters. Write this as an expression.

- David has $3p$ counters. In algebra the multiplication sign is missed out.

Collecting like terms

💡 *Remember to put the sign between, for example $5a + 2b$, not $5a$ $2b$.*

- Expressions can be simplified by collecting like terms.
- Only collect the terms if the letters and powers are identical.

Examples

$$3p + 2p = 5p$$

$6a + 2c$ cannot be simplified, since there are no like terms.

This minus sign is part of the term $2b$.

$$5n + 2n - 6n = n \text{ Note that } n \text{ means } 1n.$$

$$2a + 4b + 3a - 2b = 5a + 2b \text{ Add the } as, \text{ then the } bs.$$

$$5xy + 2yx = 7xy \text{ since } xy \text{ is the same as } yx.$$

Writing simple formulae

$n + 4$ is an expression.

$y = n + 4$ is a **formula**, since it has an = sign in it.

Example

a How many blue tiles will there be in pattern number 4?

Drawing the diagram:
There are 16 blue tiles.

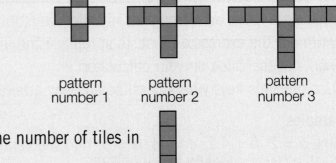

pattern number 1   pattern number 2   pattern number 3

b Write down the formula for finding the number of tiles in pattern number n.

Number of tiles $= 4 \times n + 1$
$\qquad\qquad\quad = 4n + 1$

The $4n$ is the 4 lots of blue tiles.

The $+1$ is the yellow tile in the middle.

pattern number 4

c How many tiles will be used in pattern number 12?

$n = 12$, i.e. number of tiles $= 4 \times 12 + 1$
Just substitute the value $\qquad = 48 + 1$
of n into the formula. $\qquad = 49$

> ⓘ **Remember to put an equals sign in your formula.**

KEY TERMS

Make sure you understand these terms before moving on!
- algebra
- expression
- formula
- term

❶ The diagram shows some patterns made up with sticks. If P represents the pattern number and S represents the number of sticks, write down a formula connecting S and P.

   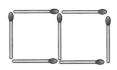   

pattern 1 　　　　 pattern 2 　　　　　　 pattern 3

❷ Write these expressions as simply as possible.

a 6 more than n 　　 **b** 4 less than p 　　 **c** 6 more than 3 lots of y
d h divided by 7 　　 **e** 5 less than n divided by p

> ⓘ **Algebra forms a large part of the SATS exam. Simple formulae like the examples shown in this chapter are very common – practise questions like these.**

Algebra 2

Substituting values into expressions and formulae

Replacing a letter with a number is called **substitution**. When substituting:
- write out the expression first, then replace the letters with the values given
- work out the value on your calculator
- Use brackets keys where possible and pay attention to **order of operations**.

Examples

Using $a = 2$, $b = 4.1$, $c = -3$, $d = 5$, find the value of each expression.
Give your answer to 1 decimal place.

a $\dfrac{a + b}{2}$ **b** $\dfrac{a^2 + c^2}{d}$ **c** ab **d** $3d - ab$

a $\dfrac{a + b}{2} = \dfrac{2 + 4.1}{2} = 3.05 = 3.1$ (1 dp)   *Remember to show the substitution.*

b $\dfrac{a^2 + c^2}{d} = \dfrac{2^2 + (-3)^2}{5} = 2.6$ 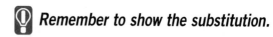 You may need to treat c^2 as $(-3)^2$ depending on your calculator.

c $ab = 2 \times 4.1 = 8.2$ ⟵ ab means $a \times b$.

d $3d - ab = (3 \times 5) - (2 \times 4.1) = 6.8$

Example

The formula $F = 1.8C + 32$ is used to change temperature in degrees Celsius (C) to temperature in degrees Fahrenheit (F). If $C = 20$, work out the value of F.

$F = 1.8C + 32$ ⟵ Substitute $C = 20$ into the formula.
$\quad = 1.8 \times 20 + 32 = 68$ Note $1.8C$ means $1.8 \times C$.

💡 *Show each step in your working.*

Multiplying letters and numbers

- Algebraic expressions are often simplified by being multiplied together, eg $5a \times 2b = 10ab$.
- When multiplying expressions, multiply the numbers together, then multiply the letters together.

💡 *There are a lot of rules/techniques to learn here. When substituting values into formulae be sure to do it carefully and show full working.*

Examples
Simplify these expressions.

Multiply the numbers.

a $3a \times 4b = 3 \times 4 \times a \times b$
$\quad = 12ab$

Multiply the letters.

b $5a \times 3b \times 2c = 5 \times 3 \times 2 \times a \times b \times c$
$\quad = 30abc$

c $2a \times 3a = 2 \times 3 \times a \times a$
$\quad = 6a^2$

Remember $a \times a = a^2$.

Multiplying out single brackets

- This helps to simplify algebraic expressions.
- Multiply everything inside the brackets by everything outside the brackets.

Examples

This is known as **expanding brackets**.

$2(a + b) = 2a + 2b$ $3(x - 2) = 3x - 6$

The multiplication sign is not shown.

$a(b + d) = ab + ad$ $r(3r - 2s) = 3r^2 - 2rs$

Remember, $r \times r = r^2$.

If the term outside the brackets is negative, all of the signs of the terms inside the brackets are **changed** when multiplying out.

Examples $-2(a + b) = -2a - 2b$ $-a(a - b) = -a^2 + ab$

To simplify expressions, expand the brackets first, then collect like terms.

- Remember, $-(a + b)$ means $-1 \times (a + b)$.

Example

$3(a + 1) + 2(a + b) = 3a + 3 + 2a + 2b$ Multiply out brackets.

$= 5a + 2b + 3$ Collect like terms.

Factorising (putting brackets in)

This is the reverse of expanding brackets.
An expression is put into brackets by taking out common factors.

expanding
$2(x + 4)$ $2x + 8$
factorising

Examples

Factorise: **a** $5x + 10 = 5(x + 2)$ **b** $8x - 16 = 8(x - 2)$ **c** $3x + 9 = 3(x + 3)$

Remember, you need to take out the highest common factor.

8 is the highest common factor of 8 and 16, not 4!

QUICK TEST

1 Simplify these expressions:
   a $5a + 2a + 3a$ **b** $6a - 2b + 5b$ **c** $3xy + 2yx$
   d $5a \times 2b$ **e** $3a \times 4a$ **f** $6a + 2b - 2b + b$

2 Some cards have the following expressions written on them.
   A $2a + 8$ **B** $2a + 4$ **C** $4a + 8$ **D** $4a + 2$
   Which card is the same as $4(a + 2)$?

3 If $a = 3$, $b = 2.1$, $c = -4$, work out the values of these expressions, giving each answer to one decimal place. **c**
   a $3a + 2b$ **b** $5c - 2a$ **c** abc

KEY TERMS

Make sure you understand these terms before moving on!
- substitution
- factorise

31

Equations 1

Solving simple linear equations

- An **equation** involves an unknown value which has to be worked out.
- The **balance method** is usually used; whatever is done to one side of an equation must be done to the other.

Examples

Solve the following.

a $n - 4 = 6$
     $n = 6 + 4$ Add 4 to both sides.
     $n = 10$

b $n + 2 = 8$
     $n = 8 - 2$ Subtract 2 from both sides.
     $n = 6$

c $5n = 20$
     $n = \dfrac{20}{5}$ Divide both sides by 5.
     $n = 4$

d $\dfrac{n}{3} = 2$
     $n = 2 \times 3$ Multiply both sides by 3.
     $n = 6$

 Show all working and do the calculation step by step.

Solving equations of the form $ax + b = c$

Examples   Solve these equations.

a $5n + 1 = 11$ Subtract 1 from both sides.
     $5n = 11 - 1$
     $5n = 10$
     $n = \dfrac{10}{5} = 2$ Divide both sides by 5.

b $\dfrac{n}{3} + 1 = 4$
     $\dfrac{n}{3} = 4 - 1$
     $\dfrac{n}{3} = 3$
     $n = 3 \times 3$ Multiply both sides by 3.
     $n = 9$

Equations are very popular on the SATS paper – try to work through them in a logical way, showing full working. If you have time, check your answer by substituting it back into the original equation.

Solving linear equations of the form $ax + b = cx + d$

The trick with this type of equation is to get the x-terms together on one side of the equals sign and the numbers on the other side.

Example

Solve this equation.

$$7x - 2 = 2x + 13$$
$$7x - 2 - 2x = 13 \qquad \text{Subtract } 2x \text{ from both sides.}$$
$$5x = 13 + 2 \qquad \text{Add 2 to both sides.}$$
$$5x = 15$$
$$x = \frac{15}{5} = 3$$

Solving linear equations with brackets

Just because an equation has brackets don't be put off – the method is just the same as for the other equations once the brackets have been multiplied out.

Examples

a
$$5(2x - 1) = 10$$
$$10x - 5 = 10 \qquad \text{Multiply brackets out first.}$$
$$10x = 10 + 5$$
$$10x = 15$$
$$x = \frac{15}{10} = 1.5$$

Or
$$5(2x - 1) = 10$$
$$2x - 1 = \frac{10}{5}$$
$$2x - 1 = 2$$
$$2x = 2 + 1$$
$$2x = 3$$
$$x = \frac{3}{2} = 1.5$$

b
$$4(2n + 5) = 3(n + 10)$$
$$8n + 20 = 3n + 30 \qquad \text{Multiply brackets out first.}$$
$$8n + 20 - 3n = 30$$
$$5n = 30 - 20$$
$$5n = 10$$
$$n = \frac{10}{5} = 2 \qquad \text{Solve as before.}$$

KEY TERMS

Make sure you understand these terms before moving on!
- equation
- balance method
- solve

QUICK TEST

Solve the following equations.

1. $2x = 10$
2. $2x - 3 = 9$
3. $4x + 1 = 8$
4. $5x + 3 = 2x + 9$
5. $6x - 1 = 2x + 15$
6. $3(x + 2) = x + 4$
7. $2(x - 1) = 6(2x + 2)$

Equations 2

Solving cubic equations by trial and improvement

Solving **cubic equations** by **trial and improvement** means making successive approximations in order to get closer to the correct value.

Example

The equation $x^3 - 5x = 10$ has a solution between 2 and 3.
Find this solution to two decimal places (2 dp).

💡 *Make sure you write down the solution for x, not the answer to $x^3 - 5x$.*

Draw a table to help.
Substitute different values of x into $x^3 - 5x$.

x	$x^3 - 5x$	Comment
2.5	3.125	too small
2.8	7.952	too small
2.9	9.889	too small
2.95	10.922375	too big
2.94	10.712184	too big
2.91	10.092171	too big

At this stage the solution is trapped between 2.90 and 2.91.
Checking the middle value $x = 2.905$ gives $x^3 - 5x = 9.99036...$ which is too small.

```
    2.90              2.905              2.91
 (too small)       (too small)        (too big)
```

The diagram makes it clear that the solution is 2.91 correct to two decimal places.

💡 *When solving equations by trial and improvement you must give the value of x which is the solution.*

Using equations to solve problems

Example

Class 9A were playing a number game. Saima said, 'Multiplying my number by 5 and adding 8 gives the same answer as subtracting my number from 20.'

a Call Saima's number y and form an equation.

$$5y + 8 = 20 - y$$

b Solve the equation to work out Saima's number.

$$5y + 8 = 20 - y$$
$$5y + 8 + y = 20$$
$$6y = 20 - 8$$
$$6y = 12$$
$$y = \frac{12}{6} = 2$$

Saima's number is 2.

> 💡 **Check at the end that $y = 2$ works in the equation.**

Example

The lengths of the sides of the triangle are given in the diagram below.

a Write down an expression for the perimeter of the triangle.

b If the perimeter of the triangle is 39 cm, form an equation and solve it to find the length of each side.

a Perimeter $= (x + 2) + (3x - 3) + (2x + 4)$
$$= 6x + 3$$

b
$$6x + 3 = 39$$
$$6x = 39 - 3$$
$$6x = 36$$
$$x = \frac{36}{6}$$
$$x = 6$$

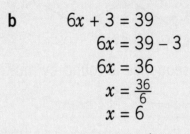

The sides are $\quad x + 2 = 8\,\text{cm}$
$$2x + 4 = 16\,\text{cm}$$
$$3x - 3 = 15\,\text{cm}$$

To find the perimeter, add the three lengths.

QUICK TEST

1 If $12x - x^2 = 34$ has a solution between 4 and 5, use trial and improvement to find the value of x to one decimal place. **C**

2
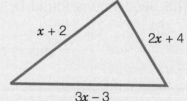

a Write down an equation for the perimeter of the rectangle above, if the perimeter is 74 cm.

b Solve the equation to find the length and width of the rectangle.

Number patterns & sequences

Number patterns and sequences

- A **sequence** is a list of numbers. There is usually a relationship between the numbers. Then the sequence forms a **number pattern**. Each number in the list is called a **term**.
- There are lots of different number patterns. To find a missing number in the number pattern it is sensible to see what is happening in the gap.

Examples

a The odd numbers have a **common difference** of 2.

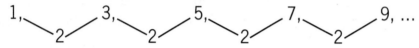

1,   3,   5,   7,   9, ...
    2   2   2   2

The rule is to add 2 each time.

b The next term in this sequence is found by multiplying the previous term by 3.

2,   6,   18,   54, ...
    ×3   ×3   ×3

c The next term in this sequence is found by adding the two previous terms.

1,   1,   2,   3,   5,   8,   13

   1 + 1   2 + 3   5 + 8

This is called the fibonacci sequence.

Dividing by 2, 5 and 10

One number is **divisible** by another if there is no remainder.

Examples

a 4 is divisible by 2,
$4 \div 2 = 2$

b 7 is not divisible by 2,
$7 \div 2 = 3.5$

- A number is divisible by 2 if it is an even number.
- A number is divisible by 5 if it ends in 0 or 5.
- A number is divisible by 10 if it ends in 0.

Function machines

Example
When the numbers are fed into this function machine,

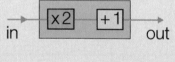

in   ×2   +1   out

they are multiplied by 2 and the result is added to 1.

- If 1 is fed in, 3 comes out ($1 \times 2 + 1 = 3$)
- If 2 is fed in, 5 comes out ($2 \times 2 + 1 = 5$)
- If 3 is fed in, 7 comes out ($3 \times 2 + 1 = 7$)
- If 4 is fed in, 9 comes out ($4 \times 2 + 1 = 9$)

This transformation can be illustrated with a mapping diagram, like this.

$1 \to 3$
$2 \to 5$
$3 \to 7$
$4 \to 9$

To describe the mapping, write $x \to 2x + 1$.
This is read as 'x becomes $2x + 1$'.

Common number patterns

1, 4, 9, 16, 25, ...	Square numbers
1, 8, 27, 64, 125, ...	Cube numbers
1, 3, 6, 10, 15, ...	Triangular numbers
1, 1, 2, 3, 5, 8, 13, ...	Fibonacci sequence
2, 4, 8, 16, 32, 64, ...	Powers of 2
10, 100, 1000, 10000, 100000, ...	Powers of 10

 These number patterns are common and you need to remember them.

Finding the nth term of a linear sequence

- The nth term is often shown as U_n, so the 12th term is U_{12}.
- For a linear sequence the nth term takes the form of $U_n = an + b$.
  The gap or difference gives the value of a.

Example
Find the nth term of this sequence.
4, 7, 10, 13, 16, ...

- Look at the differences between the terms.
  If they are the same this gives the **multiple** or a.
- Adjust the rule by adding or taking away.

term	1	2	3	4	5	... n
sequence	4	7	10	13	16	

differences: 3   3   3   3

The multiple is 3, which gives $3n$.
If n is 1, $3 \times 1 = 3$ but the first term is 4 so add 1.

$$n\text{th term } U_n = 3n + 1$$

Check your rule with the second term to make sure it works.

Example
Find the nth term of this sequence.
1, 6, 11, 16, 21, ...

term	1	2	3	4	5
sequence	1	6	11	16	21

differences: 5   5   5   5

- The multiple is 5, so 5 will be in each term.
- Now adjust the rule.
  If n is 1, $5 \times 1 = 5$ but the first term is 1 so subtract 4.

$$n\text{th term } U_n = 5n - 4$$

 Finding the nth term is a very useful method since it helps you to find a formula when given a sequence of values.

KEY TERMS

Make sure you understand these terms before moving on!

- sequence
- number pattern
- term
- common difference
- divisible

QUICK TEST

Find the nth term of each of these sequences.

1   a 5, 7, 9, 11, 13

b 3, 7, 11, 15, 19

c 8, 11, 14, 17, 20

2   Find the next two numbers in this sequence.
32, 16, 8, 4,__, __,

Coordinates & graphs

Coordinates

- **Coordinates** are used to locate the position of a point on a grid.
- When reading coordinates, read **across** first, then **up or down**.
- Coordinates are always written inside **brackets**, with a **comma** in between, i.e. (2, 4).
- The horizontal axis is the x-axis.
  The vertical axis is the y-axis.

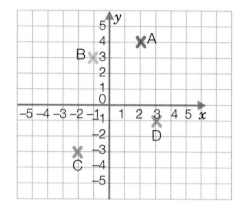

  A has coordinates (2, 4).
  B has coordinates (–1, 3).
  C has coordinates (–2, –3).
  D has coordinates (3, –1).

> *Make sure you write the brackets and comma.*
> *Remember to read across first, then up or down.*

Finding the gradient of a straight line

- To find the **gradient**, or **slope**, choose two points.
- Draw a triangle as shown.
- Find the change in y (height) and the change in x (base).
- Gradient = $\dfrac{\text{change in } y}{\text{change in } x}$ or $\dfrac{\text{height}}{\text{base}} = \dfrac{5 - 1}{3 - 0} = \dfrac{4}{3} = 1\frac{1}{3}$
- Decide if the gradient is positive or negative.

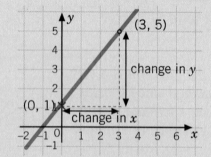

> *Do not count the squares as the scales may be different.*

KEY TERMS

Make sure you understand these terms before moving on!

- coordinates
- x-axis
- y-axis
- gradient
- parallel lines
- slope
- linear
- same

Graphs of the form $y = mx + c$

The general equation of a straight-line or **linear** graph is $y = mx + c$.

m is the gradient (steepness) of the line.

c is the intercept on the y-axis, where the graph cuts the y-axis.

Parallel lines have the **same** gradient.

Example

Draw the graphs of $y = 2x$, $y = -2x$, $y = 3x$ and $y = x - 2$ on the same axes.

- Work out coordinates for each graph.
- Plot each set of coordinates and join up the points with a straight line.
- Label each of the graphs.

$y = 2x$

x	-2	-1	0	1	2
y	-4	-2	0	2	4

$y = -2x$

x	-2	-1	0	1	2
y	4	2	0	-2	-4

$y = 3x$

x	-2	-1	0	1	2
y	-6	-3	0	3	6

$y = x - 2$

x	-2	-1	0	1	2
y	-4	-3	-2	-1	0

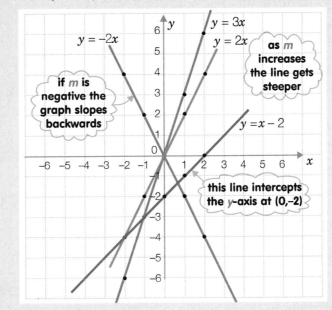

as m increases the line gets steeper

if m is negative the graph slopes backwards

this line intercepts the y-axis at (0,–2)

> Putting the coordinates in a table makes it easier.

> To work out the coordinates for the graph either:
> - draw up a table as shown in the examples, or
> - use a function machine or mapping diagrams.
> Once you have plotted the coordinates, check they are on a straight line.
> If not, check that you have worked out the coordinates properly.

1 What are the coordinates of the points A, B, C, D, E and F?

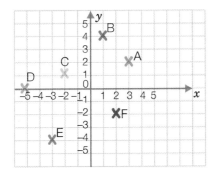

2 The graph of $y = x - 1$ is drawn on the grid. Draw the following graphs on the same axes.

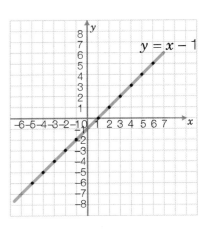

a $y = 2x$

b $y = 4x$

c What do you notice about the graphs of $y = 2x$ and $y = 4x$?

d Without working out any coordinates draw the graph of $y = x - 2$.

More graphs

Graphs of the form $y = ax^2 + b$

- These are **curved graphs**.

Example

Draw the graph of $y = x^2 - 2$.

x	−3	−2	−1	0	1	2	3
y	−7	2	−1	−2	−1	2	7

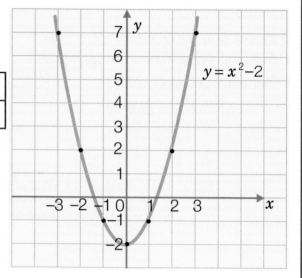

$y = x^2 - 2$

- Work out the y-coordinate for each point.

- Remember that x^2 means x times x.

- Just replace x in the equation to find each y-coordinate.

$$x = -3 \quad \text{so } y = (-3)^2 - 2 = 7$$

- The table represents the coordinates of the graph. The coordinates can now be plotted to form the graph.

- Join up the points with a smooth curve and label the graph.

- If you are asked to draw the graph of $y = 2x^2$, remember this means $y = 2 \times (x^2)$ [square x first then multiply by 2].

  Use a calculator to help work out the coordinates.

  Try to join the points with a smooth curve and use a sharp pencil.

  Take care when drawing curved graphs. Go through all the points and check for any that look wrong.

point obviously wrong

Direction of the curve

If the number in front of x^2 is **positive** the curve looks like this:

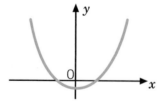

If the number in front of x^2 is **negative** the curve looks like this:

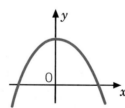

Graphs of the form $y = a$, $x = b$

Examples

a Draw the line $y = 3$.

$y = a$ is a **horizontal** line with every y-coordinate equal to a.

b Draw the line $x = 2$.

$x = b$ is a **vertical** line with every x-coordinate equal to b.

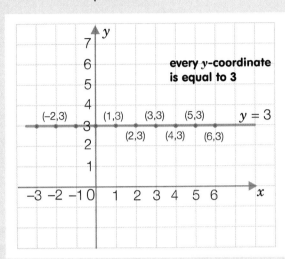

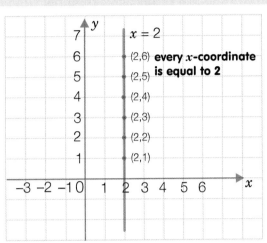

The graph of $y = x^3$

To draw the graph of $y = x^3$, follow the methods as shown before.
- Work out the y-coordinate for each point.
- Replace x in the equation with the coordinate.

x	–3	–2	–1	0	1	2	3
y	–27	–8	–1	0	1	8	27

- Plot the x- and y-coordinates from the table above.
- Notice the shape of the graph of $y = x^3$.

 Remember, $x^3 = x \times x \times x$.

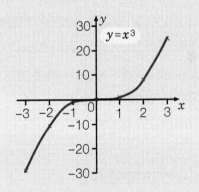

QUICK TEST

Draw the graph of $y = 2x^2 + 1$ for values of x from –3 to 3. Complete the table of values first.

x	–3	–2	–1	0	1	2	3
y	19						

Using linear graphs

Using linear graphs

- **Linear graphs** are often used to show relationships.

Examples
The graph shows the charges made by a van hire firm.
- Point A shows the basic charge for hiring the van, which is £50.
- The gradient shows that £20 was then charged per day. Hence for 5 days' hire, the van cost £50 + £20 × 5 = £150.

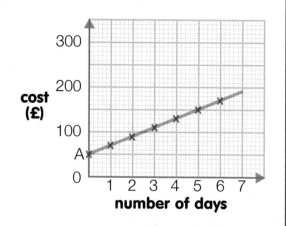

All these graphs are useful for looking at linear relationships. It is sensible to draw lines on your graph to help show how you obtained your answers.

Graphs in practical situations 1

Conversion graphs
These are used to convert values of one quantity to another, for example, litres to pints, kilometres to miles, pounds to dollars.

Example
Suppose £1 is worth $1.50.
Draw a conversion graph.

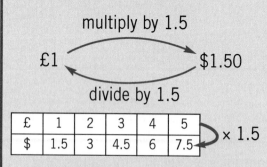

multiply by 1.5

£1 $1.50

divide by 1.5

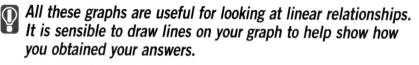

£	1	2	3	4	5
$	1.5	3	4.5	6	7.5

× 1.5

- Make a table of values.
- Plot each of these points on the graph paper.
- To change dollars to pounds, read across to the line then down, so $4 is approximately £2.67.
- To change pounds to dollars, read up to the line then read across, so £4.50 is approximately $6.80.

Graphs in practical situations 2

Distance–time graphs

Distance–time graphs are often known as **travel graphs**.

Distance is always on the vertical axis; time is always on the horizontal axis.

The speed of an object can be found from a distance–time graph by using:

$$\text{speed} = \frac{\text{distance travelled}}{\text{time taken}}$$

Example

The graph shows Mr Roger's car journey. Work out his speed at each stage of the journey.

a For the first stage of the journey:

$$\text{speed} = \frac{\text{distance}}{\text{time}} = \frac{30}{1} = 30 \text{ mph}$$

car travels at 30 mph for 1 hour.

b The car is stationary for 30 minutes.

c The graph is steeper so the car is travelling faster.

$$\text{speed} = \frac{\text{distance}}{\text{time}} = \frac{30}{0.5} = 60 \text{ mph}$$

d The car is stationary for 1 hour.

e For the return journey the speed is

$$\text{speed} = \frac{\text{distance}}{\text{time}} = \frac{60}{1.5} = 40 \text{ mph}$$

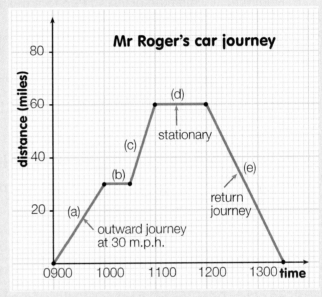

Mr Roger's car journey

Always check you understand the scales on the graph before starting a question.

Remember, 30 minutes is 0.5 hours.

When answering questions involving distance–time graphs try to keep the following in mind.

- The steeper the graph the greater the speed. Object A is travelling faster than object B which, in turn, is travelling faster than object C

- The green line shows an incorrect journey home because you cannot go back in time.

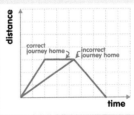

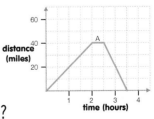

QUICK TEST

The distance–time graph shows Mrs Roberts' car journey.

a At what speed did she travel for the first 2 hours?

b What is Mrs Roberts doing at A?

c At what speed is her return journey?

Practice questions

Use the questions to test your progress. Check your answers on page 88.

1. For each of the patterns below write down the next number in the sequence.

   a 2, 4, 6, ... **b** 1, 4, 7, 10, ... **c** 2, 4, 8, 16, ... **d** 64, 32, 16, 8, ...

2. Which of these sentences are correct?

   a Numbers that end in a 2 are divisible by 2.

   b Numbers that end in a 0 are only divisible by 10.

   c Numbers in which the digits add up to a multiple of 3 are divisible by 3.

3. Complete the missing numbers from the function machines.

   a 5 → [+3] → ....

   b 7 → [×3] → ....

   c .... → [÷3] → 4

   d 9 → [+1] → [×5] → ....

4. Write these expressions as simply as possible.

   a 5 more than r ....

   b 7 less than y ....

   c p divided by 4 ....

   d 4 less than r, divided by s ....

5. Simplify these expressions.

   a $7a - 2a + a$ ....

   b $6x + 3y - 4x$ ....

   c $4cd - 2dc$ ....

   d $3p \times 5r$ ....

   e $5x \times 4x$ ....

   f $12p + 4q - 8p + q$ ....

6. A shape has the lengths shown in the diagram. Write down an expression for the perimeter of the shape. ....

   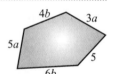

7. Here is a pattern made up of regular hexagons of side length 1 cm.

   a Complete this table showing the pattern number and perimeter of the shapes.

   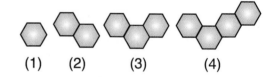

Pattern number (n)	1	2	3	4	5	6
Perimeter of shape (p)	6		14			

   (1)   (2)   (3)   (4)

   b Write down a formula that connects the perimeter (p) and the pattern number (n).

   ....

8. If $a = 3$, $b = 2$ and $c = -1$, calculate the value of each of the following.

   a $a + b + c$ ....

   b $2a - 3b$ ....

   c $5a - 2c$ ....

   d $a^2 + c^2 - 2b$ ....

9. Use the formula $v = u + at$.

   a Calculate v when $u = 200$, $a = 30$ $t = 4$. ....

   b Calculate v when $u = 500$, $a = 40$ $t = 10$. ....

10. From the expressions on these cards, find which is the same as each of thise below.

$2n + 8$	n^2	$2n + 4$	$2n$	$5n$	$4n + 8$	$2n - 2$	$2n - 1$	$n + n$	$4n + 2$

    a $4(n + 2)$ ....

    b $n \times n$ ....

    c $2(n - 1)$ ....

    d $2n + 2n - 3 + 5$ ....

11. Solve the following equations:

   a $n - 6 = 10$ ....   **b** $2n = 12$ ....

   c $5a + 10 = 15$ ....   **d** $\frac{n}{5} - 1 = 6$ ....

12. The graph of $y = x - 2$ is drawn on the graph opposite.
   Draw the following graphs on the same axes.

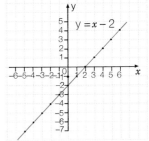

   a $y = 2x$ **b** $y = 3x$

   c What do you notice about the graphs of $y = 2x$ and $y = 3x$?

   ....

   d Without working out any coordinates, draw the graph of $y = 2x - 4$.

13. Solve the following equations.

   a $6n + 2 = 4n + 8$ ....

   b $6(n + 2) = 5n + 7$ ....

   c $2(n - 1) = 3(n + 4)$ ....

14. A rectangle has a length of $(2n + 1)$ cm and a width of 4 cm.

   a Write an expression for the perimeter of the rectangle. Simplify as much as possible.

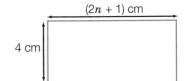

   ....

   b If the perimeter of the rectangle is 22 cm, write an equation involving n and solve it to find the value of n.

   ....

15. Write down the nth term of the sequence 5, 7, 9, 11, 13, ...

16. Factorise the following expressions.

   a $5x + 15$ ....

   b $6x - 12$ ....

   c $12x + 20$ ....

17. For each function write down the gradient and intercept of its line.

   a $y = 4x + 10$ ....   **b** $y = 6 - 2x$ ....

18. The travel graph shows the car journeys of two people.
   From the travel graph find:

   a the speed at which Miss Young is travelling ....

   b the length of time Mr Price has a break

   c the speed of Mr Price from London to Birmingham

   d the time at which Miss Young and Mr Price pass each other.

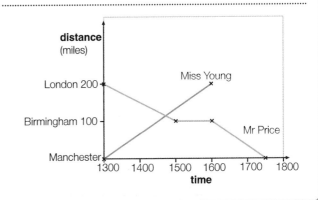

Shapes

Polygons

Polygons are 2D shapes with straight sides.
Regular polygons are shapes with all sides equal and all angles equal.

 Try to learn all the shapes and their symmetrical properties.

Number of sides	Name of polygon
3	triangle
4	quadrilateral
5	pentagon
6	hexagon
7	heptagon
8	octagon

Regular pentagon
- Five equal sides
- Rotational symmetry of order 5
- Five lines of symmetry

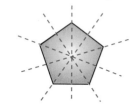

Regular hexagon
- Six equal sides
- Rotational symmetry of order 6
- Six lines of symmetry

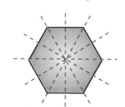

Regular octagon
- Eight equal sides
- Rotational symmetry of order 8
- Eight lines of symmetry

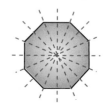

Quadrilaterals

Quadrilaterals are four-sided shapes.

Square
- Four lines of symmetry
- Rotational symmetry of order 4

Rectangle
- Two lines of symmetry
- Rotational symmetry of order 2

Parallelogram
- No lines of symmetry
- Rotational symmetry of order 2

Rhombus
- Two lines of symmetry
- Rotational symmetry of order 2

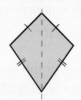

Kite
- One line of symmetry
- No rotational symmetry

Trapezium

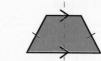
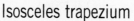

Isosceles trapezium
- One line of symmetry
- No rotational symmetry

Trapezium
- No lines of symmetry
- No rotational symmetry

 You need to be able to sketch these shapes and know their symmetry properties.
Parallel lines are lines that remain the same distance apart, they never meet.

Triangles

There are several types of triangle.

Right-angled
- Has a 90° angle

Equilateral
- Three sides equal
- Three angles equal

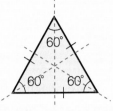

Isosceles
- Two sides equal
- Base angles equal

Scalene
- No sides the same
- No angles the same

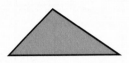

The circle

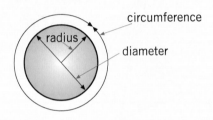

An angle in a semicircle is always a **right angle**.

Diameter = 2 × radius
The **circumference** is the distance around the outside edge.

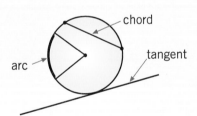

The **perpendicular bisector** of a chord passes through the centre of a circle.

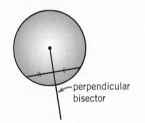

- A **chord** is a line that joins two points on the circumference.
- A diameter is a chord that goes through the centre.
- A **tangent** touches the circle at one point only.
- An **arc** is part of the circumference.

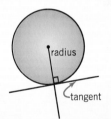

The radius and tangent at a point make an angle of 90°.

QUICK TEST

1. What is the name of a six-sided polygon?
2. From memory, draw all the main triangles and quadrilaterals.

Solids

3D shapes

A **prism** is a solid that can be cut into slices that are all the same shape and size. These shapes are all prisms.

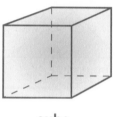 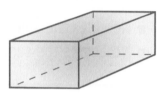 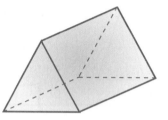 

| cube | cuboid | triangular prism | cylinder |

These shapes are not prisms.

 You need to know the names of all these solids.

cone   **sphere**   square-based pyramid

Nets of solids

The **net** of a 3D shape is the 2D (flat) shape, that can be folded to make the 3D shape.

Examples

cuboid

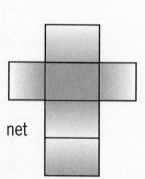

net

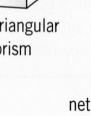

triangular prism

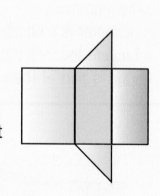

net

 When you need to draw an accurate net, you must measure all the lengths carefully. When you make the shape, remember to put tabs on the net, to stick it together.

Faces, edges and vertices

A **face** is a flat surface of a solid.
An **edge** is where two faces meet.
Vertex is another word for a corner.
The plural is **vertices**.
A cuboid has six faces, eight vertices and 12 edges.

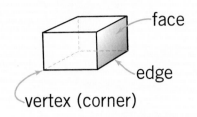

 Edges that cannot be seen are usually shown with dotted lines.

Plans and elevations

A **plan** is what is seen if a 3D shape is viewed from above.
An **elevation** is what is seen if the 3D shape is viewed from the side or front.

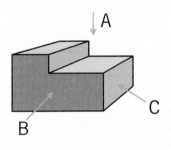

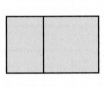
plan A

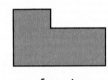
front
elevation B

side
elevation C

KEY TERMS

Make sure you understand these terms before moving on!

- prism
- cube
- cuboid
- triangular prism
- cylinder
- cone
- sphere
- square-based pyramid
- net
- face
- edge
- vertex
- plan
- elevation

QUICK TEST

1. Draw an accurate net of this 3D shape.

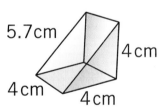

5.7cm 4cm
4cm 4cm

2. Draw a sketch of the plan and elevations from A and B of this solid.

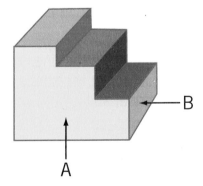

Symmetry

Reflective symmetry

- If a shape has **reflective symmetry**, both sides of the shape are symmetrical when a mirror line is drawn across it. The mirror line is known as the **line** or **axis of symmetry**.

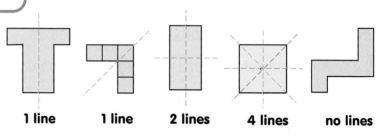

1 line   1 line   2 lines   4 lines   no lines

Example

Half a reflected shape is shown here. The dashed line is a line of symmetry. Copy and complete the shape.

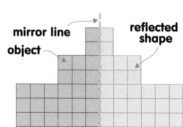

mirror line
object
reflected shape

Rotational symmetry

- A 2D (two-dimensional) shape has **rotational symmetry** if, when it is turned about its centre, it looks exactly the same. The **order of rotational symmetry** is the number of times the shape turns and looks the same.

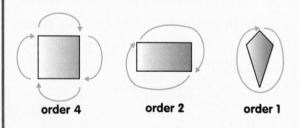

order 4   order 2   order 1

The kite has one position. It has **rotational symmetry of order 1** or **no** rotational symmetry.

Plane symmetry

Plane symmetry occurs only in 3D (three-dimensional) solids.
A 3D shape has a plane of symmetry if the plane divides the shape into two halves, and one half is the exact mirror image of the other.

plane of symmetry

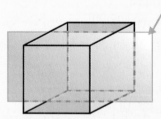

ⓘ *When drawing a plane of symmetry on a solid, remember to make it a 'closed' shape and not just a line of symmetry.*

1. The dotted lines are the lines of symmetry. Complete the shape so that it is symmetrical about both lines.

2. What are the names of the three types of symmetry?

3. Draw a plane of symmetry on this solid.

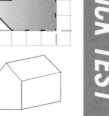

KEY TERM

Make sure you understand these terms before moving on!
- axis of symmetry
- reflective symmetry
- rotational symmetry
- plane symmetry
- order of rotational symmetry

Constructions & LOGO

Constructing a triangle

Example: Use compasses to construct this triangle.
- Draw the longest side.
- With the compass point at A, draw an **arc** of radius 4 cm.
- With the compass point at B, draw an arc of radius 5 cm.
- Join A and B to the point where the two arcs meet at C.

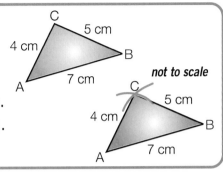

Bisecting an angle

- Draw two lines XY and YZ to meet at an angle.
- Place the compass point at Y and draw two arcs, one on XY and one on YZ.
- Placing the compass point on the arcs on XY and YZ in turn, draw arcs to cross at N. Join Y to N.

YN is the **bisector** of angle XYZ.

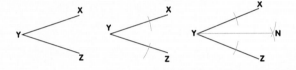

LOGO

- This computer program is used to draw shapes.
- It can also show transformations.

The instructions to draw an equilateral triangle:

FORWARD 4
TURN RIGHT 120°
FORWARD 4
TURN RIGHT 120°
FORWARD 4

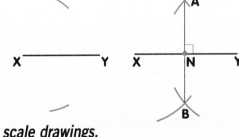

Perpendicular bisector of a line

- Draw a line XY.
- With X as the centre, use compasses to draw two arcs. The compasses must be set at a radius greater than half the distance of XY.
- With Y as the centre and the compasses set at the same radius, raw two more arcs.
- Join the two points where the arcs cross.
- AB is the **perpendicular bisector** of XY.
- N is the **midpoint** of XY.

Constructions are useful when answering questions on scale drawings.

QUICK TEST

1. Shape A is a rectangle. Complete the LOGO commands for drawing the rectangle:
FORWARD 2
TURN RIGHT 90°
FORWARD 5

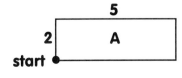

Angles & tessellations

Angles and the protractor

An **angle** is an amount of turning or rotation. Angles are measured using a **protractor**, in **degrees**. A circle can be divided into 360 parts. Each part is one degree and this is written as 1°.

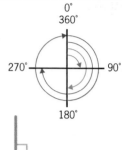

An **acute** angle is between 0° and 90°.

An **obtuse** angle is between 90° and 180°.

A **reflex** angle is between 180° and 360°.

A **right angle** is 90°.

Measuring angles using a protractor

Lay the protractor over the angle with its base along one side of the angle. For this angle measure on the outer scale since you must start from 0°.

Read from 0° on the outer scale.

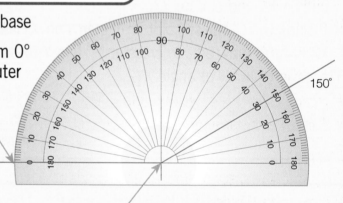

150°

 Be sure to put the 0° line at the start position and read from the correct scale.
When measuring angles, count the degree lines carefully and always double check.

Place the cross at the point of the angle you are measuring.

Angle facts

Angles on a **straight line** add up to **180°**.
$a + b + c = 180°$

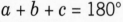

Angles at a **point** add up to **360°**.
$a + b + c = 360°$

Angles in a **triangle** add up to **180°**.
$a + b + c = 180°$

Angles in a **quadrilateral** add up to **360°**.
$a + b + c + d = 360°$

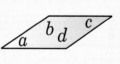

Vertically opposite angles are equal.
$a = b, c = d$
$a + c = b + d = 180°$

An **exterior angle** of a triangle equals the sum of the two opposite **interior angles**.
$a + b = c$

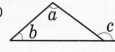

 You must remember these angle facts as you will need to apply them to questions.

Angles in parallel lines

Alternate (Z) angles are **equal**.

Corresponding angles are **equal**.

Supplementary angles add up to **180°**. $c + d = $ **180°**.

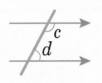

Reading angles

Angle ABC or ∠ABC or $\hat{ABC}$ is the angle shown by the middle letter, in this case B.

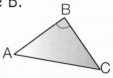

Angles in polygons

The two types of angle in a polygon: **interior** (inside) and **exterior** (outside).

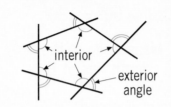

For a regular polygon with n sides:

- Sum of exterior angles = 360°
  So exterior angle = $\dfrac{360°}{n}$
- Interior angle + exterior angle = 180°
- Sum of interior angles = $(n - 2) \times 180°$

Example

Calculate the interior and exterior angle of a regular pentagon.

A pentagon has 5 sides, i.e. $n = 5$

Exterior angle = $\frac{360}{5}$ = 72°

Interior angle + exterior angle = 180°

Interior angle = 180° − 72° = 108°

Angle questions

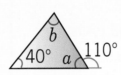

$a + 110° = 180°$
$a = 70°$
$70° + 40° + b = 180°$
$b = 180° − 110° = 70°$

$a = 70°$ (alternate)
$b = 70°$ (corresponding)
$c = 70°$ (corresponding to a)
$d = 180° − 70° = 110°$
(angles on a straight line)

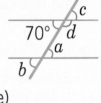

❗ *Always show full working when carrying out an angle calculation.*

KEY TERMS

Make sure you understand these terms before moving on!

- angle
- protractor
- acute
- obtuse
- reflex
- alternate
- corresponding
- supplementary
- exterior angle
- interior angle

Tessellations

- A tessellation is a pattern of 2D shapes which fit together without leaving any gaps.
- For shapes to tessellate, the angles at each point must add up to 360°.

Example

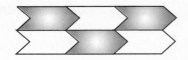

❶ Find the size of the angles labelled by letters.

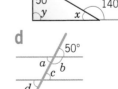

❷ Find the size of **a** an exterior and **b** an interior angle of a regular hexagon.

Bearings & scale drawings

Compass points

The diagram shows the points of the compass.

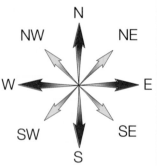

Example

If Paulo is facing east and turns **clockwise** through an angle of 270°, what direction will he now be facing?

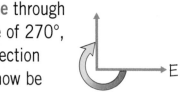

Paulo will now be facing north.

 Remember, clockwise is this direction.

Bearings

- **Bearings** give a direction in degrees.
- Bearings are always measured from the **north** in a **clockwise** direction.
- They must have three figures.

Examples

Bearing of A from B
= 180° − 50° = 130°.

Measure from the north line at B.

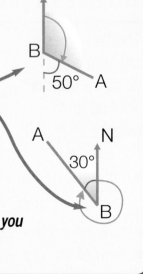

Bearing of A from B
= 360° − 30° = 330°.

 The word 'from' is very important when answering bearings questions. It tells you where to put the north line and measure from.

Scale drawings

Example

Here is a rough sketch of a sector of a circle. Using a scale of 1 cm to 2 m, draw an accurate drawing of the sector.

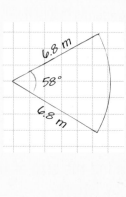

A scale of 1 cm to 2 m means that 6.8 m is
6.8 ÷ 2 = 3.4 cm on the diagram.

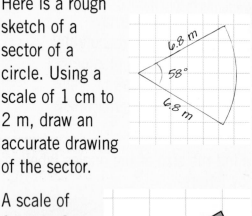

Scales and maps

Scales are often used on maps. They are usually written as a ratio.

Example

Q The scale on a road map is 1 : 25 000. Bury and Oldham are 20 cm apart on the map. Work out the real distance, in kilometres, between Bury and Oldham.

A Scale 1 : 25 000,
distance on map is 20 cm.
Real distance = 20 × 25 000 = 500 000 cm.
Divide by 100 to change cm to m:
500 000 ÷ 100 = 5000 m.
Divide by 1000 to change m to km:
5000 ÷ 1000 = 5 km.

 A scale of 1 : 25 000 means that 1 cm on the scale drawing represents a real length of 25 000 cm.

Back bearings

In the diagrams below, the **back bearing** is the bearing of B from A.
- Draw a north line at A.
- Use the properties of parallel lines, since both north lines are parallel.

Examples

Bearing of B from A
$= 360° - 50°$
$= 310°$.

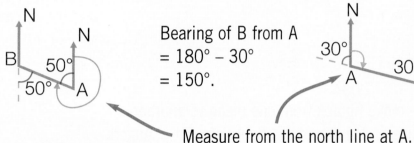

Bearing of B from A
$= 180° - 30°$
$= 150°$.

Measure from the north line at A.

 Look for alternate (Z) or corresponding angles.

Scale drawings and bearings

Scale drawings are very useful for measuring lengths which cannot be measured directly.

Example

A ship sails from a harbour for 15 km on a bearing of 040°, and then continues due east for 20 km. Make a scale drawing of this journey using a scale of 1 cm to 5 km. How far will the ship have to sail to get back to the harbour by the shortest route?
What will the bearing be?

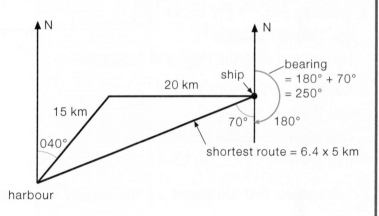

Shortest route = 6.4 × 5 km = 32 km. Bearing = 70° + 180° = 250°.

KEY TERMS

Make sure you understand these terms before moving on!
- compass
- clockwise
- bearing
- back bearing
- scale

QUICK TEST

① What are the bearings of X from Y in the following?

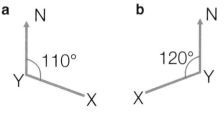

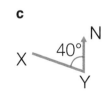

② For each of the questions above work out the bearings of Y from X.

Transformations

- A transformation changes the position or size of a shape.
- There are four types of transformation: translation, reflection, rotation and enlargement.

Translations

- These move figures from one place to another.
- The size and shape of the figure are not changed.

Vectors are used to describe the distance and direction of the **translation**.

A vector is written as $\begin{pmatrix} a \\ b \end{pmatrix}$.

a represents the **horizontal** movement, and b represents the **vertical** movement.

Example

a Translate ABC by the vector $\begin{pmatrix} 2 \\ 1 \end{pmatrix}$.
  Call the new triangle P.
  This means 2 to the right and 1 upwards.

b Translate ABC by the vector $\begin{pmatrix} -3 \\ -2 \end{pmatrix}$.
  Call the new triangle Q.
  This means 3 to the left and 2 down.

P and Q are **congruent** to each other and to ABC.

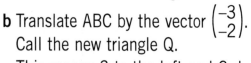

> Remember that two shapes are congruent if one is exactly the same as the other.

Reflections

Reflections create an image of an object on the other side of a mirror line. The mirror line is known as an **axis of reflection**. The size and shape of the figure are not changed.

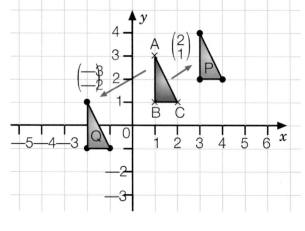

Example

Reflect triangle ABC in:

a the x-axis, and call it D

b the line $y = -x$, and call it E

c the line $x = 5$, and call it F.

D, E and F are congruent to triangle ABC.

> Count the squares to find the distance of the object from the mirror.

Rotations

Rotations turn a figure through an angle about some fixed point.
This fixed point is called the **centre of rotation**.
The size and shape of the figure are not changed.

Example

Rotate triangle ABC:

a 90° clockwise about (0, 0) and call it R

b 180° about (0, 0), and call it S

c 90° anticlockwise about (–1, 1), and call it T.

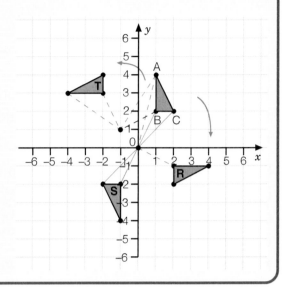

When describing a rotation give the centre of rotation, the direction of the turn (clockwise/anticlockwise) and the angle of the turn.

Enlargements

- **Enlargements** change the size but not the shape of an object.
- The **centre of enlargement** is the point from which the enlargement takes place.
- The **scale factor** indicates how many times longer each length of the original figure becomes.
- If the scale factor is **greater than 1**, the shape becomes **bigger**.
- If the scale factor is **less than 1**, the shape becomes **smaller**.

Example

Enlarge shape ABCDEF by a scale factor of 2, centre (0, 0).
Call it A'B'C'D'E'F'.

Notice that each side of the enlargement is twice the length of the original. OA' = 2 × OA.

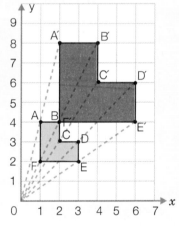

If asked to describe an enlargement, state the centre of enlargement and the scale factor.

KEY TERMS

Make sure you understand these terms before moving on!

- vector
- translation
- axis of reflection
- centre of rotation
- rotation
- enlargement
- centre of enlargement
- scale factor
- congruent
- reflection

QUICK TEST

1 On the diagram on the right:

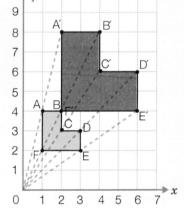

a Translate ABC by the vector $\begin{pmatrix} -3 \\ 1 \end{pmatrix}$.
Call it P.

b Reflect ABC in the line $y = x$.
Call it Q.

c Reflect ABC in the line $y = -1$.
Call it R.

d Rotate ABC 180° about (0, 0). Call it S.

Measures & measurement 1

Estimating measures

Estimates using metric and imperial units need to be made all the time.

- **Metric** units include kilometres (km), metres (m), kilograms (kg).
- **Imperial** units include miles, yards, pounds, pints.

Estimating lengths

Lengths and distances can be measured using these types of units.

- **Metric**: kilometres (km), metres (m), centimetres (cm) and millimetres (mm)
- **Imperial**: feet, inches, yards and miles

Some common estimates include:

- a door is about 2 metres high or about $6\frac{1}{2}$ feet.

- a 30 cm ruler is about 1 foot long.

o   30 cm

Estimating capacities

Capacity is a measure of how much a container can hold.

- **Metric**: millilitres (ml), centilitres (cl), litres (l)
- **Imperial**: gallons, pints

Some common estimates include:

- a 1 pint milk carton holds about 570 ml.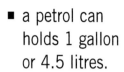

- a petrol can holds 1 gallon or 4.5 litres.

  Petrol can 1 gallon

- a can of pop holds about 300 ml or $\frac{1}{2}$ pint.

  COLA

Estimating weights (masses)

Weights can be measured in these units.

- **Metric**: milligrams (mg), grams (g), kilograms (kg), tonnes (t)
- **Imperial**: ounces (oz), pounds (lb), stones, tons

Some common estimates are:

- a 1 kg bag of sugar weighs about 2.2 lb.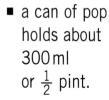

  SUGAR

- a 500 g packet of butter weighs about 1 lb.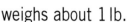

Reading scales

Decimals are usually used when reading off scales. Measuring jugs, rulers and weighing scales are all examples of scales which use decimals.

Examples

8.2   8.6
8   8.5   9

There are 10 spaces between the 8 and the 9. Each space is 0.1.

6.2   6.6
6   7

There are five spaces between the 6 and the 7. Each space is 0.2.

12.25 12.75 13.5
12   13   14

There are four spaces between the 12 and 13. Each space is 0.25.

Metric units

Length
10 mm = 1 cm
100 cm = 1 m
1000 m = 1 km

Weight
1000 mg = 1 g
1000 g = 1 kg
1000 kg = 1 tonne

Capacity
1000 ml = 1 litre
100 cl = 1 litre
1000 cm³ = 1 litre

Converting units
- If changing from **small** units to **large** units (e.g. g to kg) **divide**.
- If changing from **large** units to **small** units (e.g. km to metres) **multiply**.

Examples   500 cm = 5 metres (÷ 100)   5 litres = 500 cl (× 100)
3500 g = 3.5 kg (÷ 1000)   25 cm = 250 mm (× 10)

 Try to remember these metric equivalents.

Imperial units

Length
12 inches = 1 foot
3 feet = 1 yard

Weight
16 ounces (oz) = 1 pound
14 pounds (lb) = 1 stone

Capacity
20 fluid oz = 1 pint
8 pints = 1 gallon

Comparisons between metric and imperial units

Length
2.5 cm ≈ 1 inch
30 cm ≈ 1 foot
1 metre ≈ 39 inches
8 km ≈ 5 miles

Weight
25 g ≈ 1 ounce
1 kg ≈ 2.2 pounds

Capacity
1 litre ≈ $1\frac{3}{4}$ pints
4.5 litres ≈ 1 gallon

Example
Change 8 inches into centimetres.
1 inch ≈ 2.5 cm   8 inches ≈ 8 × 2.5 = 20 cm

- *Check to see if your answer sounds sensible.*
- *You need to learn the metric and imperial conversions. To help you remember them, try learning with a friend and testing each other.*

KEY TERMS

Make sure you understand these terms before moving on!
- metric
- imperial
- length
- weight
- capacity
- mass

QUICK TEST

1. Change 6200 g into kg.
2. Change 4.2 cm into mm.
3. Change 6 litres into pints.
4. What do the pointers on the scales represent?
5. The weight of a newborn baby could be about:

   a 50 g   b 5 g   c 3 kg   d 30 kg

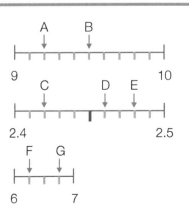

Measures & measurement 2

The calendar

A year has 12 months.
There are 365 days in a year.
In a leap year there are 366 days because February has 29 days in a leap year.

January	31 days	July	31 days
February	28 or 29 days	August	31 days
March	31 days	September	30 days
April	30 days	October	31 days
May	31 days	November	30 days
June	30 days	December	31 days

12- and 24-hour clock times

The **12-hour clock** uses **am**, which means **before midday**, and **pm** which means **after midday**.

The **24-hour clock** numbers the hours from 0 to 24. It is written with four figures.

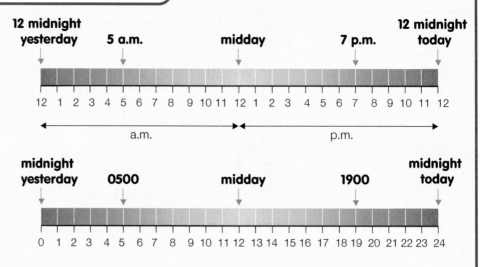

You need to be able to write times using both the 12-hour and 24-hour clock.

Examples

2:42 pm is the same as 1442.   1534 is the same as 3:34 pm.

4:30 am is the same as 0430.   0904 is the same as 9:04 am.

 Remember to write in 'am' and 'pm' for 12-hour clock times.

Time facts

There are 60 **seconds** in one minute.
There are 60 **minutes** in one hour.
There are 24 **hours** in one day.
There are 7 **days** in one week.
There are 52 **weeks** in one **year**.

This clock has two hands.
The short hand tells the hour, and the long hand tells the minutes.

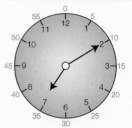

For the hour hand each mark is one hour.
For the minute hand each mark is five minutes.
This clock reads 10 past 7.

Timetables

Timetables often use 24-hour clock time. Timetables should be read carefully.

Example
The train timetable illustrates the train times from London to Manchester.

There will be a train from London every 60 minutes, at 0750, 0850.

London, Euston	0602	0650	Every 60 minutes until	1100	1300
Watford Junction	0632	0720		1130	1330
Stoke-on-Trent	0750	0838		–	1445
Manchester, Piccadilly	0838	0926		1315	1540

The 0750 train from Stoke-on-Trent

The 0650 train from London arrives in Manchester at 0926.

The 1100 from London does not stop at Stoke-on-Trent.

Q Diana is travelling from Watford Junction to Manchester, Piccadilly. If she catches the 0632 train, how long does her journey take?

A 0632   0838
Depart   Arrive   Time = 2 hours 6 minutes
Watford Junction   Manchester

Q If I arrive at London, Euston at 1142, how long do I have to wait for the next train to Manchester?

A The next train is at 1300 hours. I must wait:
1142 → 1200 = 18 minutes
1200 → 1300 = one hour   I wait one hour 18 minutes.

If the timetable is written in 24-hour clock times, make sure your answers are in 24-hour clock times.
Remember, there are only 60 minutes in 1 hour.
Reading a timetable is a very important technique. You will be expected to be able to read and interpret a selection of different timetables and charts.

KEY TERMS

Make sure you understand these terms before moving on!
- 12-hour clock
- am
- pm
- 24-hour clock
- seconds
- minutes
- hours
- days
- weeks
- year

QUICK TEST

1. A bus arrives at Bury bus station at 0830. It takes 42 minutes to travel from there to Manchester. At what time does it arrive in Manchester?

2. How many seconds are there in 3 minutes?

3. The train for Manchester leaves London at 0635. The journey takes 3 hours and 20 minutes. At what time does it arrive in Manchester?

4. Write these times using the 24-hour clock.
   a 6:32 pm   b 8:27 am
   c 2:34 am   d 9:36 pm

Area & perimeter of 2D shapes

Estimating the area and finding the perimeter of 2D shapes

Perimeter is the distance around the outside edge of a shape.

Area is the amount of space a 2D shape covers. Common units of area include square millimetres (mm^2), square centimetres (cm^2), square metres (m^2).

Example

Find the perimeter of this shape:

Perimeter = 4 + 5 + 3
        + 2.7 + 2.7
        = 17.4 cm

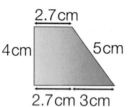
2.7 cm
4 cm
5 cm
2.7 cm 3 cm

You can estimate areas of irregular shapes by counting the squares they cover.

Example

1	2	3	4
5	6	7	8
9	10	11	12
13	14	15	16
17	18	19

these make 1 whole square

this is $\frac{1}{2}$ a square

- Label the squares as you count them.
- Try to match up parts of squares to make up wholes.

The shape has an area of 20.5 units^2.
It is cm^2 when each square is 1 cm^2.

Areas of quadrilaterals and triangles

Area of a rectangle

Area = length × width

$A = l \times w$

width

length

Area of a triangle

$A = \frac{1}{2} \times$ base × perpendicular height

$A = \frac{1}{2} \times b \times h$

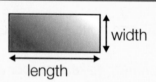
perpendicular height

base

Area of a trapezium

$A = \frac{1}{2} \times$ (sum of parallel sides)
    × perpendicular height between sides

$A = \frac{1}{2} \times (a + b) \times h$

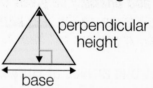
height h
a
b

💡 **Remember to work out the brackets first.**

Area of a parallelogram

Area = base × **perpendicular height**

$A = b \times h$

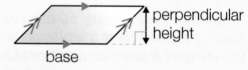
perpendicular height

base

Examples

Find the area of the following shapes.

$A = \frac{1}{2} \times b \times h$

$A = \frac{1}{2} \times 7 \times 5$

  $= 17.5 \, cm^2$

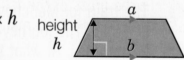
5 cm
7 cm

$A = \frac{1}{2} \times (a + b) \times h$

$A = \frac{1}{2} \times (10 + 8) \times 5$

  $= 45 \, cm^2$

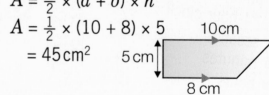
10 cm
5 cm
8 cm

Circumference and area of a circle

Circumference = π × diameter

$$C = \pi \times d$$
$$= 2 \times \pi \times \text{radius}$$
$$= 2 \times \pi \times r$$

Area = π × (radius)²

$$A = \pi \times r^2$$

Example

Find the circumference and area of this circle. (Use π = 3.14.)

$$C = \pi \times d$$
$$= 3.14 \times 10$$
$$= 31.4 \text{ cm}$$

$A = \pi \times r^2$ ($r = 10 \div 2 = 5$)

$$A = 3.14 \times 5^2$$
$$= 78.5 \text{ cm}^2$$

10 cm

💡 *Remember that the circumference of a circle is the distance around the outside edge.*
Remember r^2 means $r \times r$.

Example

Mohammed's bicycle wheel has a diameter of 60 cm.
Work out the circumference of the wheel, using π = 3.14.

$$C = \pi \times d$$
$$C = 3.14 \times 60$$
$$C = 188.4 \text{ cm}$$

If Mohammed travels a distance of 50 metres on the
bicycle, how many times does his wheel turn around?
Change 50 m into cm first: 50 × 100 = 5000 cm
Distance ÷ circumference = number of turns

$$\frac{5000}{188.4} = 26.5 \text{ times}$$

The wheel must turn 27 times for Mohammed to go a distance of 50 metres.

💡 *Always check that the units are the same before beginning a question on area or perimeter.*
Check that you have written the units for your answer as you may be awarded marks for this.
Try your best to learn all your formulae because you will only be given the formula for the area
of a trapezium on the 4–6 paper. No formulae are given on the 3–5 paper.
Use π = 3.14 or the value of π on your calculator, if you are not told its value in the question.
Check that the answer is sensible.

KEY TERMS

Make sure you understand these terms before moving on!

- perimeter
- area
- perpendicular height
- circumference
- diameter
- radius

QUICK TEST

❶ Work out the areas of the following shapes, giving your answers to one decimal place if necessary. Use π = 3.14. **C**

a ⬜ 9 cm, 3 cm   b △ 6cm, 12 cm   c ◢ 5cm, 3cm, 8cm   d ⬤ 5cm

❷ Work out the circumference of a circle with a radius of 4.9 cm. Use π = 3.14. **C**

Volume of 3D solids

Estimating volumes

Volume is the amount of space a 3D solid occupies.

Common units of volume include cubic millimetres (mm^3), cubic centimetres (cm^3), cubic metres (m^3).

The volume of a 3D solid can be found by counting how many centimetre cubes would fit into it.

Example

This cube has a volume of $1\,cm^3$ (1 cubic centimetre).

The volume of this shape is $24\,cm^3$.

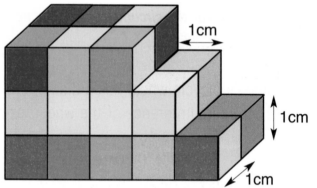

Volume of a prism

Volume = area of cross-section × length
$$V = A \times l$$

A **prism** is any solid that can be cut into slices, that are all the same shape. This is a **uniform cross-section**.

area of cross-section — length

Example

A door wedge is in the shape of a trapezium. Work out the volume of the door wedge.

Area of cross-section:

$$A = \frac{(a + b)}{2} \times h$$

$$A = \frac{(3 + 8)}{2} \times 5 = 27.5\ cm^2$$

Volume = $27.5 \times 4 = 110\ cm^3$

💡 *Substitute values in carefully and show full working out.*

Remember, to find the volume, multiply the area of cross-section by the length.

Example

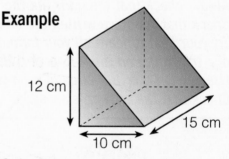

Calculate the volume of this right-angled triangular prism.

Area of cross-section:

$$A = \tfrac{1}{2} \times b \times h$$

$$A = \tfrac{1}{2} \times 10 \times 12 = 60\,cm^2$$

Volume = $60 \times 15 = 900\,cm^3$

Volumes of cubes and cuboids

Volume of a cuboid

Volume = length × width × height

$$V = l \times w \times h$$

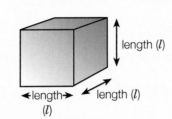

height (h)

width (w)

length (l)

Volume of a cube

Volume = length × length × length

$$V = l \times l \times l$$
$$V = l^3$$

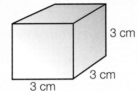

length (l)

length (l)

length (l)

Example

Find the volumes of the following shapes.

a
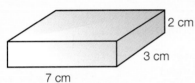
2 cm

3 cm

7 cm

Volume = $l \times w \times h$

= 7 × 3 × 2 = 42 cm³

b

3 cm

3 cm

3 cm

Volume = $l \times l \times l$

= 3 × 3 × 3 = 27 cm³

⓪ *You will need to learn the formulae for the cuboid.*

⓪ *Change all the lengths to the same units before starting! Remember to put in your units at the end.*

KEY TERMS

Make sure you understand these terms before moving on!

- volume
- uniform cross section
- cuboid
- prism
- cube

QUICK TEST

① Work out the volume of these 3D solids, giving your answer to one decimal place. Ⓒ

a
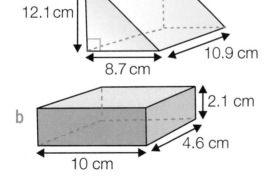

12.1 cm

8.7 cm

10.9 cm

b

2.1 cm

10 cm

4.6 cm

c

9 cm

18 cm

40 cm

② If the volume of this prism is 120 cm³, calculate the value of x. Ⓒ

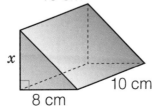

x

8 cm

10 cm

Practice questions

Use the questions to test your progress.
Check your answers on page 89.

1. Ahmed is facing south. If he turns through 90° clockwise, which direction is he now facing? ....

2. How many seconds are there in 5 minutes? ....

3. Write these times using the 24-hour clock time:

   a 8:43 am .... **b** 7:30 pm .... **c** 11:40 pm .... **d** 3:04 am ....

4. Joanne sets off for school at 7:50 am. Her journey takes her 45 minutes. At what time does she arrive at school? ....

5. How many edges does a cuboid have? ....

6. Choose the correct units from the box to complete the statements below.

cm kg km g ml l m mm

   a The thickness of a book is about 17 ....   **b** Fiona's mother weighed 52 ....

   c A giraffe is about 5 .... tall   **d** A mug holds about 250 .... of water

   e The height of the classroom would be about 3 ....

7. Write down what each of these pointers shows.

   A .... B .... C .... D .... E .... F .... G ....

8. **a** Draw the lines of symmetry on the rectangle.

   b What is the order of rotational symmetry of the rectangle?

9. Write down the order of rotational symmetry, if any, of these shapes.

10. 72°   241°   379°   127°   83°   90°   41°

    List the angles that are:

    a acute .... **b** obtuse .... **c** reflex .... **d** right-angles ....

11. Find the size of each angle marked with a letter.

    i 57° a 43°
    ii b 115°
    iii 88° 50° d c
    iv 50° e
    v f 110° 48° 100°
    vi 60° g h i

    Ⓒ A calculator may be used.

12. Each cube has a volume of 1 cm³. Calculate the volume of this shape.

    .... cm³

13. **a** Change 3.75 kg into g ....

    b Change 53 mm into cm ....

    c Change 7 pints into litres ....

14. Draw:

    a the plan of the solid

    b the elevations of the solid as seen from A and B

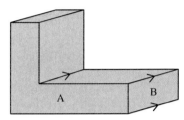

15. Work out the area of the following shapes, giving your answer to one decimal place.

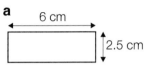 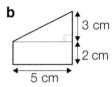

16. Work out the area of each of the following shapes.

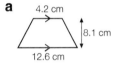 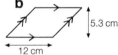 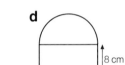

17. Work out the circumference of a circle with a radius of 4.9 cm. Use π = 3.14. **C**

18. Calculate the area of the shaded region. Use π = 3.14. **C**

19. What are the bearings of X from Y in these diagrams?

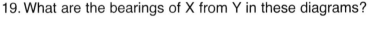

20. **a** Reflect shape A in the x axis. Call it B.

    b Rotate shape A 90° anticlockwise about (0, 0). Call it C.

    c Translate shape A by $\begin{pmatrix} -4 \\ -6 \end{pmatrix}$. Call it D.

    d Enlarge shape A by a scale factor of 2, centre of enlargement (0, 0). Call it E.

21. Work out the volume of each of these 3D shapes. **C**

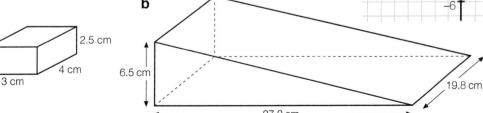

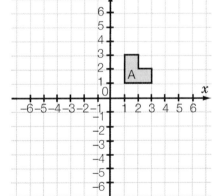

Collecting data

Types of data

- **Discrete data** can only take particular values, often found by counting. Examples include the number of red cars in a car park.
- **Continuous data** can take any value in a given range, often found by measuring. Examples include the height and weight of year 8 pupils.
- **Primary data** is data that you collect yourself.
- **Secondary data** is data that somebody else has collected, such as in a census.

Collecting information

- Data that has been collected can be sorted into a table called a **tally chart** or **frequency table**.
- The tally chart shows the frequency of each item (how often the item occurs).
- A tally is just a line I. Tallies grouped into fives are easier to count. The fifth tally forms a gate, ⊬⊬⊬.

Grouping data

If the data covers a large range of results, it is usual to group it into **class intervals**, all of the same width. For continuous data the class intervals are often written using inequalities.

Example

The heights in cm of 30 pupils were:

137	142	139	120	152	126
149	147	138	135	135	132
127	154	150	138	144	149
150	122	140	142	138	141
149	127	125	141	140	135

💡 *You may find it helpful to cross off the data as you put it in the table.*

- The data has been grouped into class intervals of 5.
- Choose sensible groupings of 2, 5 or 10.
- Check that all data has been included.

Height (h cm)	Tally	Frequency
$120 \leqslant h < 125$	II	2
$125 \leqslant h < 130$	IIII	4
$130 \leqslant h < 135$	I	1
$135 \leqslant h < 140$	⊬⊬⊬ III	8
$140 \leqslant h < 145$	⊬⊬⊬ II	7
$145 \leqslant h < 150$	IIII	4
$150 \leqslant h < 155$	IIII	4
Total		30

$120 \leqslant h < 125$ means that the heights are all at least 120 cm but less than 125 cm.

$120 \leqslant h$ means that the height can be less than or equal to 120 cm.

$h < 125$ means that the height cannot be equal to 125 cm. It would go into the next group.

💡 *Always check the total at the end to make sure all data is included.*

Surveys and questionnaires

- Data can be collected by using **questionnaires** to carry out **surveys**.
- A **hypothesis** is a prediction which can be tested and usually gives a purpose to the survey, for example, 'Most teachers have red cars'.
- An **observation sheet** is used to collect data. It must be clear and easy to use.

Questionnaires

When designing questionnaires:
- Keep the questionnaire short.
- Give instructions on how to fill it in.
- Ask questions which cover the survey's purpose.
- Do not ask for information which is not needed, such as a name.
- Make sure that your opinion is not evident, for example, 'Do you agree that *Neighbours* is better than *Home and Away*?'
- Allow for all possible outcomes.

Example

Colour of staff cars		
Colour	Tally	Frequency
red		
blue		
white		
green		
black		
others		

Example

How much do you spend on magazines each week?

| Under £1 ☐ | £1–£1.99 ☐ |
| £2 – £2.99 ☐ | £3 or over ☐ |

When asked to write a questionnaire always word your questions very carefully. Tick boxes are useful when sorting your information.

Stem-and-leaf diagrams

Stem-and-leaf diagrams are another way of recording information.

Example

The heights in cm of some students are:
154, 172, 160, 164, 168, 177, 181, 140, 142, 153, 154, 153, 162
The ordered stem-and-leaf diagram for this information would look like this.

```
14 | 0  2
15 | 3  3  4  4
16 | 0  2  4  8
17 | 2  7
18 | 1
```

For the value 142 cm the stem is 14 and the leaf is 2. To read off the values, multiply the stem by 10 and add on the leaf.

Stem = 10 cm (Key 18|1 means 181 cm)
In a stem-and-leaf diagram, all the individual values are recorded.
You can read them off the diagram.

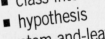

Make sure you understand these terms before moving on!
- discrete data
- continuous data
- primary data
- secondary data
- tally chart
- frequency table
- class intervals
- hypothesis
- stem-and-leaf diagrams

QUICK TEST

1. Richard and Tammy are carrying out a survey on some students' favourite foods. Design a data collection sheet that they could use.

2. Draw a stem-and-leaf diagram for this data. Use Stem = 10 and a key.
206, 241, 243, 237, 239, 231, 246, 222, 215, 214, 209, 213, 227

Representing information

Data can be shown in several ways using different types of diagrams.

All the different types of diagrams in this section as they commonly appear on SATS papers.

Bar charts and pictograms

A **bar chart** is a set of bars or columns of equal width. The height of each bar shows the frequency of the data it represents. Bar charts can be drawn with or without gaps between the bars.

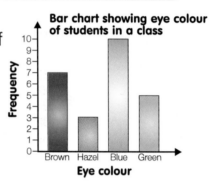

Bar chart showing eye colour of students in a class

Pictograms use symbols. Each symbol represents a certain number of items.

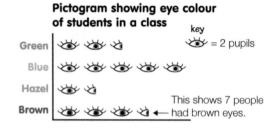

Pictogram showing eye colour of students in a class

key
👁 = 2 pupils

This shows 7 people had brown eyes.

 Bar line graphs are similar to bar charts except lines are used instead of bars.

Pie charts

Pie charts are circles split up into sections. Each section represents a category or certain number of items.

Calculating angles for a pie chart
- Find the total of all items listed.
- Find the fraction of the total for each type of item.
- Multiply the fraction by 360° to find the angle.

 Remember, there are 360° at the centre of the circle. Check that your angles add up to 360°.

Interpreting pie charts
The pie chart shows how some students travel to school.
There are 18 students in total.
How many travel by:
a car **b** bus **c** walking?

$360° = 18$ students
$1° = \frac{18}{360} = 0.05$ work out $1°$
Car $= 60 \times 0.05 = 3$ students
Bus $= 80 \times 0.05 = 4$ students
Walk $= 220 \times 0.05 = 11$ students

 Measure the angles carefully with a protractor.

Example
The table shows the favourite sports of 24 students in year 9.

Sport	Frequency
Football	9
Swimming	5
Netball	3
Hockey	7

Finding the angle

9 out of 24 like football, $\frac{9}{24} \times 360° = 135°$

Key in on the calculator:

9 ÷ 2 4 × 3 6 0 =

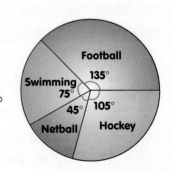

Frequency diagrams

- **Frequency diagrams** are drawn to illustrate **continuous data**.
- There are no gaps between the bars.
- The data must be grouped into equal class intervals if the heights of the bar are used to represent the frequencies.

Example
The heights of 30 pupils are grouped as shown in the table.

Height (h cm)	Frequency
$120 \leqslant h < 125$	2
$125 \leqslant h < 130$	4
$130 \leqslant h < 135$	1
$135 \leqslant h < 140$	8
$140 \leqslant h < 145$	7
$145 \leqslant h < 150$	4
$150 \leqslant h < 155$	4
	30

- The axes do not need to start at zero.
- Do not leave gaps between the bars.
- Label the axes and write a title.

Check that you've labelled the axes and written a title.

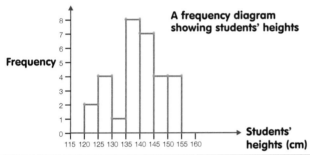

A frequency diagram showing students' heights

Using tables

Information is often presented in **tables**. It is important that you can extract the relevant information.

Example
The table shows the average height of some boys and girls in a school.

Boys' height (cm)	Age	Girls' height (cm)
117	7	117
120	8	119
121	9	122
124	10	130
132	11	138
139	12	142
148	13	150
152	14	155

a If the height of a boy is 132 cm, approximately what is his age?
age = 11 years

b At what age is the average height of the girls the same as the average height of the boys?
age = 7 years

Line graphs

A **line graph** is a set of points joined by a line. Line graphs can be used to show trends in continuous data.

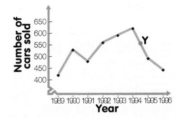

Example

Year	1989	1990	1991	1992	1993	1994	1995	1996
Number of cars sold	420	530	480	560	590	620	490	440

This can also be referred to as a time series since time is represented on the horizontal axis.

Middle values (for example point Y) have no meaning. You cannot say that halfway between 1994 and 1995, 550 cars were sold.

QUICK TEST

A manufacturer of chocolate asked 1440 students which type of chocolate they preferred. The pie chart shows the results. How many people preferred: **C**

a white chocolate
b fruit and nut
c milk chocolate?

KEY TERMS

- bar chart
- pictogram
- pie chart
- frequency diagrams
- continuous data
- line graph
- middle values

Scatter diagrams & misleading graphs

■ A *scatter diagram* (*scattergraph*) is used to show two sets of data at the same time.

■ It is used to show the connection (*correlation*) between two sets of data.

Types of correlation

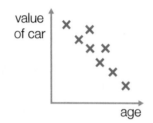

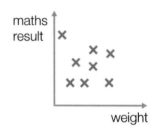

Positive correlation
As one value increases so does the other. If the points are nearly on a straight line there is **high positive correlation**.

Negative correlation
As one value increases the other decreases. If the points are nearly on a straight line there is **high negative correlation**.

Zero correlation
There is no correlation between the values.

In the KS3 SATS you must be able to describe the types of correlation.

Drawing scatter diagrams 1

■ Work out the scales first before starting. Plot the points carefully, ticking off each point in the table as it is plotted.

Example

The data shows the age of several cars and how much they are now worth.

Age (years)	1	8	4	7	6	3	5	7	3	5	2
Price (£)	5200	1200	3400	1800	2800	4000	1800	2400	4400	3000	5000

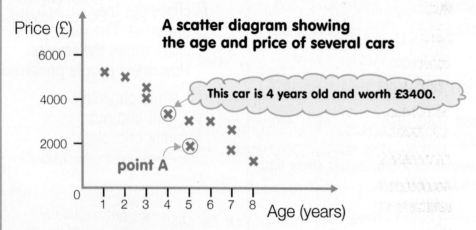

A scatter diagram showing the age and price of several cars

This car is 4 years old and worth £3400.

point A

■ The scatter diagram shows that the older the cars become the less they are worth, i.e. there is a **negative correlation**.

Drawing scatter diagrams 2

- **Point A** shows a car which is five years old and worth £1800. This is slightly less than expected and may be due to rust or a dent, or the make, etc.

 Plot the points carefully as it is easy to make mistakes.
Do not rush when drawing a scatter diagram.
You also need to be able to interpret the scatter diagram.

Misleading graphs

Statistical graphs are sometimes misleading; they do not tell the true story.

Examples

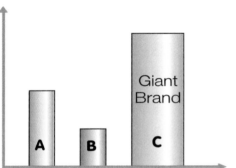

This graph has no scales and the bars are not the same width.

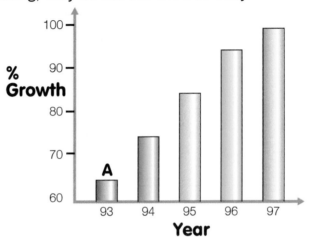

In this graph the scales do not start at zero, so the growth looks much bigger than it actually is.

Brand A
10000
sold

Brand B
20000
sold

In this pictogram the boxes do not relate to their volumes. Although Brand B has only sold twice the amount of Brand A it gives the impression of having sold much more.

 In the exam make any criticisms clear.

KEY TERMS

Make sure you understand these terms before moving on!

- scatter diagram
- scattergraph
- correlation
- negative correlation
- positive correlation
- zero correlation

QUICK TEST

Look at the two graphs.

a What does Graph 1 tell you about the relationship between the number of ice lollies sold and the temperature?

b What does Graph 2 tell you about the relationship between the number of cups of tea sold and the temperature?

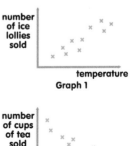

number of ice lollies sold

temperature
Graph 1

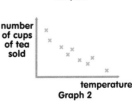

number of cups of tea sold

temperature
Graph 2

Averages 1

Averages of discrete data 1

There are three types of average: mean, median and mode.

$\text{Mean} = \dfrac{\text{sum of a set of values}}{\text{the number of values used}}$ Sometimes known as the **average**.

Median = the middle value when the numbers are put in order of size.

Mode = the one that occurs the most often.

Range = highest value − lowest value. Shows how much the information is spread.

Example

A football team scored the following number of goals in their first ten matches.

2, 4, 0, 1, 2, 2, 3, 6, 2, 4

Find the mean, median, mode and range of the number of goals scored.

Mean $= \dfrac{2+4+0+1+2+2+3+6+2+4}{10}$

$= \dfrac{26}{10} = 2.6$ goals   Do not round off.

Median   0, 1, 2, 2, 2, 2, 3, 4, 4, 6   Put in order of size first.

~~0~~ ~~1~~ ~~2~~ ~~2~~ (2 2) ~~3~~ ~~4~~ ~~4~~ ~~6~~   Count from the ends to find the middle.

If there are two numbers in the middle, the median is halfway between them.

Median $= \dfrac{2+2}{2} = 2$ goals

Mode   = 2 goals, because it occurs 4 times

Range   = 6 − 0 = 6   Remember to subtract the lowest value from the highest value.

Example

The mean of four numbers is 20, the mean of six other numbers is 36. What is the mean of all 10 numbers?

The sum of the four numbers is 80. $\left(\dfrac{80}{4} = 20\right)$

The sum of the six numbers is 216. $\left(\dfrac{216}{6} = 36\right)$

Mean of all 10 numbers is 29.6. $\left(\dfrac{\text{total sum}}{10} = \dfrac{80+216}{10} = \dfrac{296}{10} = 29.6\right)$

Averages of discrete data 2

Example

The mean of four numbers is 7. Three of the numbers are 10, 4 and 8.
Find the value of the other number.

The sum of the four numbers is 28. $\left(\frac{28}{4} = 7\right)$

If x is the missing number: $10 + 4 + 8 + x = 28$

$$22 + x = 28$$
$$x = 6$$

The other number is 6.

Example

There are three hidden cards.

The mean of the three numbers is 4.
The range of the three numbers is 4.
The median of the three numbers is 4.
What are the three numbers?

Since the median is 4, the middle card is 4.
Since the mean is 4 three cards must add up to 12 and the difference between the highest and lowest card is 4.
The three cards must be

2 **4** **6**

Using appropriate averages

- The **mean** is useful when a typical value is wanted. Be careful not to use the mean if there are extreme values, e.g. for this data 1, 2, 3, 4, 57
- The **median** is a useful average to use if there are extreme values.
- The **mode** is useful when the most common value is needed.

💡 *Averages is a common topic on the KS3 SATS. It is important that you can remember which is which!*
Median – sounds a bit like 'middle'.
Mode – sounds a bit like 'most'.

KEY TERMS

Make sure you understand these terms before moving on!
- mean
- median
- mode
- range

QUICK TEST

1. Find the mean, median, mode and range of this data. Ⓒ

   2, 4, 1, 1, 2, 3, 7, 5, 5, 5, 2, 5, 6

2. Find the mean of this data.

   1, 2, 2, 7, 4, 9

3. Find the median of this data.

   7, 1, 4, 4, 3, 3, 9

Averages 2

Finding averages from a frequency table

A **frequency table** tells you how many there are in a group.

Example

Charlotte made this frequency table for how late, in minutes, students arrived for registration.

Number of minutes late (x)	0	1	2	3	4
Frequency (f)	10	4	6	3	2

Two students were four minutes late.

This tells you that four students were one minute late for registration.

Mean

$$\text{Mean} = \frac{\text{total of the results when multiplied}}{\text{total of the frequency}}$$

$$= \frac{(10 \times 0) + (4 \times 1) + (6 \times 2) + (3 \times 3) + (2 \times 4)}{(10 + 4 + 6 + 3 + 2)}$$

$$= \frac{0 + 4 + 12 + 9 + 8}{25} = \frac{33}{25} = 1.32 \text{ minutes late}$$

Remember to add up the total frequency.

💡 *When finding the mean of a frequency table, remember to divide by the sum of the frequencies and not by the total number of groups.*

Median

There are 25 students in the class, the middle person is the 13th.
From the frequency table:

Number of minutes late (x)	0	1	2	3	4
Frequency (f)	10	4	6	3	2

The 13th student is in here.

Median number of minutes late is 1.

These are the first 10 students

Mode

This is the one that has the highest frequency.
Mode = 0 minutes late because its frequency is higher than any others.

Remember to write down the answer zero, not the number 10 (this is the frequency).

Range = 4 − 0 = 4 minutes.

Comparing sets of data

The **range** and averages are used to compare sets of **data**.

Example

Class 9A obtained a mean of
57% in a test.
Class 9T obtained a mean of 84%
in the same test.

From the averages you might say 9T
did better than 9A.
However, looking at the range for each class:

$$9A = 100\% - 21\% = 79\%$$
$$9T = 94\% - 76\% = 18\%$$

Using the range it can be seen that not all of 9T did better than 9A, because some of 9A obtained higher marks than 9T. The average for 9A has been lowered because of the low marks obtained by some pupils.

Use the range when comparing data.

Example

Mia and Jack kept a record of all their maths test marks. They worked out their mean mark and their range, the results are shown in the table below.

	Mean score	Range
Mia	56%	27%
Jack	54%	14%

Comment on these results.

From these results we can see that Mia's average mark is higher but Jack has a smaller range. This shows that Jack was more consistent.

KEY TERMS

Make sure you understand these terms before moving on!
- frequency table
- range
- data

QUICK TEST

① The numbers of sisters that students in class 9M have are recorded in the table below. **c**

Number of sisters (x)	0	1	2	3	4	5	6
Frequency (f)	7	9	4	4	2	2	1

   a Calculate the mean number of sisters that the students have.

   b What is the modal number of sisters?

② Find the mean of this information in this table. **c**

x	0	1	2	3	4
Frequency (f)	12	20	40	22	6

Probability 1

What is probability?

- **Probability** is a measure of how likely that it is that something will happen.
- A probability must be written as a **fraction**, **decimal** or **percentage**. Never write the words 'out of'.
- Probabilities can be shown on a **probability scale**. All probabilities lie in the range 0 to 1. No event has a probability greater than 1.

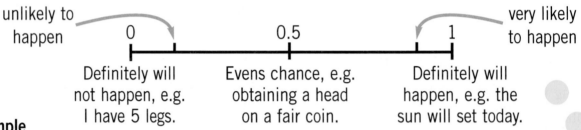

unlikely to happen — 0 — 0.5 — 1 — very likely to happen

Definitely will not happen, e.g. I have 5 legs.

Evens chance, e.g. obtaining a head on a fair coin.

Definitely will happen, e.g. the sun will set today.

Example

A bag contains three red, one blue and four yellow beads. A bead is chosen at random.
a Mark with an X the probability of choosing a green bead.
b Mark with a Y the probability of choosing a yellow bead.

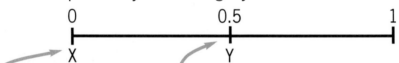

0 — 0.5 — 1
X — Y

X is at 0 since there are no green beads, i.e. a green will definitely not be chosen.

A yellow bead has an evens chance of being chosen, since half of the beads are yellow.

Exhaustive events account for all possible outcomes. The list 1, 2, 3, 4, 5, 6 gives all possible outcomes when a fair die is thrown. Throwing the die is an **event**.

Probability of an event not happening

If two events cannot happen at the same time:

P(event will not happen) =
1 – P(event will happen)

To find the probability that an event will not happen:

- Find the probability the event will happen.
- Subtract it from 1.

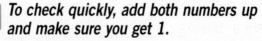
To check quickly, add both numbers up and make sure you get 1.

Example
The probability that it will rain today is $\frac{7}{11}$. What is the probability that it will not rain?
P(not rain) = 1 – P(will rain)
P(not rain) = $1 - \frac{7}{11} = \frac{4}{11}$

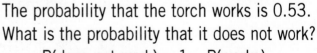

Example
The probability that the torch works is 0.53. What is the probability that it does not work?
P(does not work) = 1 – P(works)
P(does not work) = 1 – 0.53 = 0.47

Probability in practice

- Estimates of probability can be carried out by experiment or surveys.

Example 1

Based on the results of a survey we could estimate the probability that the next car to pass the school is silver.

Calculating probabilities

- Some probabilities can be calculated using the fact that each outcome is equally likely.

Probability of an event = $\dfrac{\text{number of ways an event can happen}}{\text{total number of outcomes}}$

P(event) is the shortened way of writing the probability of an event.

Example 2

There are 12 socks in a drawer: three are red, four are pink and blue and the rest are black. Nigel picks out a sock at random. What is the probability that the sock he has pulled out is:

a pink and blue   **b** red   **c** black   **d** pink and blue, red or black   **e** green?

a P(pink and blue) = $\frac{4}{12}$ = $\frac{1}{3}$

b P(red) = $\frac{3}{12}$ = $\frac{1}{4}$

Make sure that the number on the bottom is the total number of outcomes.

c P(black) = $\frac{5}{12}$

All probabilities add up to 1, since choosing a pink and blue, red or black sock will definitely happen.

d P(pink and blue, red or black) = $\frac{12}{12}$ = 1

e P(green) = 0

There are no green socks in the drawer so the event will definitely not happen.

 Whenever you do a question on probability, check that your answer is not greater than 1. If it is you've done it wrong, so go back and try again.

KEY TERMS

Make sure you understand these terms before moving on!
- probability
- probability scale
- exhaustive events

QUICK TEST

1 On the number line below, place the arrows on the scale to show these probabilities.
  a I will obtain a head or tail if I throw a fair coin.
  b I will grow wings by 6 pm today.
  c I will get an even number if I throw a fair die.

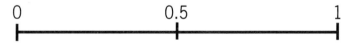

```
0                    0.5                    1
├─────────────────────┼─────────────────────┤
```

2 A bag has three red, four green and ten yellow beads in it. If Reece takes out a bead at random, what is the probability that it is:
  a a red bead   b a green bead   c a red or green bead
  d a pink bead   e a red, green or yellow bead?

3 The probability that Annie leaves a message on an answering machine is 0.32. What is the probability that she does not leave a message?

Probability 2

Possible outcomes for two or more events

- Using lists, diagrams and tables is helpful when there are outcomes of two events.

Example (lists)

For his lunch Matthew can choose a main course and a pudding.
List all the possible outcomes of his lunch.

Menu	
Main Courses	**Puddings**
Pizza	Apple pie
Chicken	Lemon tart
Salad	

Pizza, Apple pie   Chicken, Apple pie   Salad, Apple pie
Pizza, Lemon tart   Chicken, Lemon tart   Salad, Lemon tart
There are 6 possible outcomes.

Try to write out the outcomes in a well-ordered way.

Example (sample space diagram)

The spinner and the die are thrown together, and their scores are added.
Represent the outcomes on a **sample space diagram**.

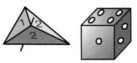

- There are 18 outcomes.

a P(score of 6) $= \frac{3}{18} = \frac{1}{6}$

b P(multiple of 4) $= \frac{5}{18}$

Spinner

2	3	④	5	⑥	7	⑧
2	3	④	5	⑥	7	⑧
1	2	3	④	5	⑥	7
1	2	3	4	5	6	

Die

2 on the spinner, 6 on the die, 2 + 6 = 8

It may help to put rings or squares around the numbers you need.

Example (two-way table)

The diagram shows a two-way table for pupils in a class who are studying either French or German.

a If a person is chosen at random, what is the probability that they do French?

$$P(\text{French}) = \frac{24}{34} = \frac{12}{17}$$

Language	Male	Female	Total
French	7	17	24
German	4	6	10
Total	11	23	34

b If a girl is chosen at random, what is the probability that she does German?

$$P(\text{German}) = \frac{6}{23}$$

Six girls do German.
There are 23 girls in total.

Example (tree diagram)

On a tree diagram, probabilities are written on the branches, and multiplied to obtain the final probabilities.
The probability that Carlos is late for registration is 0.3. Find the probability that Carlos is late on both days.
The probability that Carlos is late on both days is 0.09.

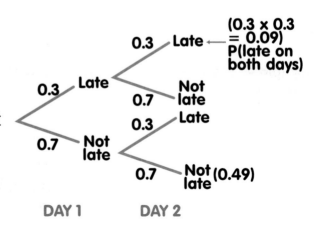

(0.3 x 0.3 = 0.09)
P(late on both days)

DAY 1   DAY 2

Expected number

- Probability can be used to estimate the expected number of times an event is likely to occur.

Example 1

If a die is thrown 180 times, approximately how many times am I likely to throw a 2?

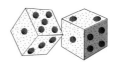

Remember there are six outcomes on a die.

$P(2) = \frac{1}{6} \times 180 = 30$ times

Since a 2 is expected $\frac{1}{6}$ of the time.

Key in on the calculator: $\boxed{1}\,\boxed{\div}\,\boxed{6}\,\boxed{\times}\,\boxed{1}\,\boxed{8}\,\boxed{0}\,\boxed{=}$

or: $\boxed{1}\,\boxed{8}\,\boxed{0}\,\boxed{\div}\,\boxed{6}\,\boxed{=}$

Example 2

The probability that Ellie obtains full marks in a spelling test is 0.4. If she takes 30 spelling tests in a year, in how many tests would you expect her to make no mistakes?

$0.4 \times 30 = 12$ tests

Example 3

The probability that John hits a bull's eye with a dart is 40%. How many times does John expect to hit the bull's eye if he throws 300 darts?

$40\% = 0.4$

$0.4 \times 300 = 120$ times

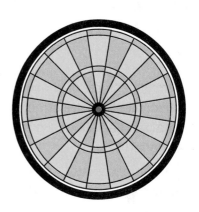

KEY TERMS

Make sure you understand these terms before moving on!
- sample space diagram
- two-way table
- tree diagram

QUICK TEST

1. The probability that you pass a driving test on the first attempt is 0.35. If 200 people are taking a driving test, how many would you expect to pass first time?

2. Two fair dice are thrown together and their totals multiplied. Complete the sample space diagram.

   Die 1

	1	2	3	4	5	6
6						12
5						
4						24
3			6		15	
2			4			
1	1			4		

   Die 2

   a What is the probability of a total of 12?

   b What is the probability that the total is a multiple of 4?

3. There are three pens in a bag: red, green and black. Write down the possible combinations if two pens are chosen at random.

Practice questions

Use the questions to test your progress. Check your answers on page 90.

1. The frequency table shows the hair colour of 20 pupils.

Hair colour	Brown	Black	Auburn	Blonde
Frequency	9	6	3	2

   a Draw a pictogram of this information. Let 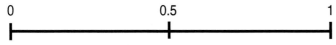 represent 2 pupils.

   b Draw a bar chart of this information.

2. On the number line below, place arrows on the scale to show these probabilities.

   a I will obtain an even number if I throw a fair die.

   b I will have two wings by 5 pm today.

   c I will obtain a number from 1 to 6 if I throw a fair die.

3. Write down an event which has a probability of 0.

   ....

4. Write down an event which has a probability of 1.

   ....

5. A manufacturer of chocolate asked 200 students which type of chocolate they preferred.
   The pie chart shows the results. Write down how many students preferred:

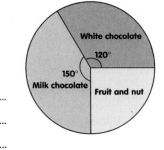

   a white chocolate ....

   b fruit and nut ....

   c milk chocolate ....

6. The letters M A T H E M A T I C S are placed on separate pieces of card and these are put into a bag. Reece picks out a card at random. What is the probability that he picks:

   a a letter T ....

   b a letter M ....

   c the letter A or C? ....

7. A bag has four red, three green and two yellow counters.
   A counter is chosen at random. Write down the probability that it is:

   a red ....

   b yellow ....

   c green or yellow ....

   d black ....

8. Find the mean, median, mode and range of this data. Ⓒ
   2, 4, 1, 1, 2, 3, 7, 5, 5, 5, 2, 5, 6

   ....

9. The table shows how many sisters some students had.

Sisters	0	1	2	3	4
Frequency	5	15	9	2	1

Calculate the mean number of sisters. Give your answer to two decimal places. **C**

10. The probability that I receive a letter is 32%. What is the probability that I do not receive a letter?

....

11. The probability that it rains on any particular day in August is $\frac{2}{}$.
What is the probability that it will not rain?

....

12. **a** Describe the correlation in the scatter diagram.

   b Rupinder got 40 marks on test 2. Approximately how many marks did she get on test 1?

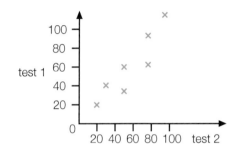

13. The probability of passing a driving test is 0.7.
If 200 people take the test today, how many would you expect to pass?

....

14. The diagram shows a two-way table for pupils in a class, who are studying either Italian or Spanish.

	Male	Female	Total
Italian	5	10	15
Spanish	12	4	16
Total	17	14	31

   a If a person is chosen at random, what is the probability that they do Spanish?

....

   b If a girl is chosen at random, what is the probability that she does Italian?

....

15. This question was included in a survey. 'Do you agree that swimming lessons should only take place on a Saturday morning?' What is wrong with the question?

....

16. The probability that a bus is late is 0.4. By drawing a tree diagram or otherwise, calculate the probability that the bus is late on two consecutive days.

....

How well did you do?   X   1–4 **Try again**   5–8 **Getting there**   9–13 **Good work**   14–16 **Excellent!** ✓

Practice questions

Use the questions to test your progress.
Check your answers on page 90.

1. If Tuesday is the 19th May, what day will the 27th May fall on?

2. Linda earns £22.50 per hour for her part-time job. If she works for 8 hours, how much does she get paid?

3. For each of these statements, decide on the correct metric units.

    a A teaspoon holds about 5 .... of medicine.

    b Terry weighs about 70 ....

    c The distance from London to Bristol is measured in ....

4. Work out the answers to these questions. Show your working.

    a 53 × 7 ....

    b 162 ÷ 9 ....

    c 813 − 354 ....

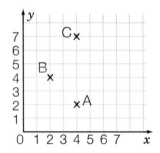

5. Write down the coordinates of A, B and C
    Plot the point D so that the shape formed when the points are
    joined up is a square. What are the coordinates of D? ....

6. The temperature in Birmingham last night was −3°C. If the temperature rises by 12 degrees, what is the temperature now?

    ....

7. A box of chocolates contains 15 hard centres and 13 soft centres.
    One chocolate is chosen at random; work out the probability that it will be:

    a a hard centre ....

    b a soft centre ....

    c a mint ....

8. On the square, draw on all the lines of symmetry.
    What is the order of rotational symmetry? ....

9. Imran has a bag of s sweets. Write an expression for each of the following.

    a Jonathan has four more sweets than Imran. ....

    b Susan has twice as many sweets as Imran. ....

    c Matthew has half as many sweets as Jonathan. ....

10. Solve the following equations.

   c $2x + 10 = 22$ ....

   c $5x - 1 = 3x + 11$ ....

11. Work out angles a, b, c, d and e.

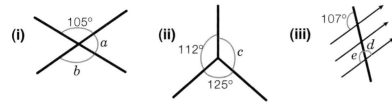

12. Work out the answers.

   a 493 × 78 ....

   b $45\overline{)1215}$ ....

13. The probability that Emily misses the bus is $\frac{7}{}$.

   What is the probability that she does not miss the bus?

   ....

14. Kelly says that when she spins the spinner, the probability that she gets a 4 is $\frac{1}{}$.
   Why is she wrong?

   ....

15. Charlotte carried out a survey to find out the favourite flavours of crisps in her class.
   The results are shown in the table below. **C**

Crisp flavour	Frequency
Cheese	7
Salt 'n' vinegar	10
Beef	6
Smoky bacon	1

   Draw a pie chart of this information.

16. The 'Good Shoe Shop' is having a sale: '30% off everything'. Calculate the sale price of a pair
   of shoes costing £40. **C**

   ....

17. Write down the nth term of this sequence.

   7, 10, 13, 16, … ....

18. Work out the volume of this 3D solid, giving
   your answer correct to one decimal place. **C**

   ....

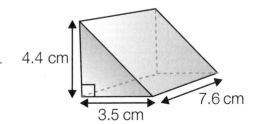

C A calculator may be used.

19. Mr Riches shares £125 000 between his two sisters in the ratio 11 : 14. Work out how much each receives.

....

20. Sketch the graphs of:

a $y = 3x - 4$

b $y = 4 - 2x$

Write down the gradient and intercept of each one.

21. If $a = 4$, $b = 3.2$ and $c = 6.5$, evaluate the expression $a^2b + 2c$. Ⓒ

....

22. The table shows the numbers of goals scored (x) during the football season. Calculate the mean number of goals scored during the football season.

x	0	1	2	3
Frequency	30	42	21	17

....

23. The equation $x^3 - 5x = 10$ has a solution between 2 and 3. By using a trial and improvement method, find the solution to one decimal place.

....

....

....

....

....

....

....

....

....

....

....

....

....

....

....

How well did you do?   ✗   1–6 **Try again**   7–12 **Getting there**   13–17 **Good work**   18–23 **Excellent!**   ✓

Number
Quick test answers

Page 5 Numbers 1
1. 10, 12, 14, 16, 18, 20
2. 24, 30, 36
3. Twenty-seven thousand, four hundred and two

Page 7 Numbers 2
1. a) 3, 6, 9, 12   b) 2, 3, 5, 7, 11
   c) 1, 2, 4, 5, 10   d) 2, 4, 6, 8, 10, 12   e) 5, 10
2. a) 10   b) 64   c) 8   d) 8
3. HCF = 5   LCM = 100

Page 9 Positive & negative numbers
1. 7°C
2. a) $A = 15$ b) $B = 4$ c) $C = 4$
   d) $D = -10$ e) $E = -10$ f) $F = -20$

Page 11 Working with numbers
1. a) 705   b) 491   c) 2208   d) 255
2. 13 113
3. 25
4. a) 152   b) 630   c) 21 000 d) 0.252
5. £12.24 6. 13

Page 13 Fractions
1. a) $x = 24$ b) $y = 25$ c) $z = 152$
2. a) $\frac{1}{3}$ b) $\frac{7}{20}$ c) $\frac{6}{13}$ d) $1\frac{1}{3}$
3. 15 pupils

Page 15 Decimals
1. a) 170.97   b) 3.84   c) 83.4
   d) 15.7
2. a) 146   b) 1257   c) 3210
   d) 0.97   e) 2.71   f) 0.026
3. a) 0.03, 0.037, 0.62, 0.84
   b) 22.507, 22.53, 27.06, 27.064

Page 17 Percentages
1. 3   2. 35   3. 40
4. 22.6%   5. 82%   6. £51
7. 36 people

Page 18 Equivalents
1.

Fraction	Decimal	Percentage
$\frac{3}{4}$	0.75	75%
$\frac{2}{5}$	0.4	40%
$\frac{1}{3}$	$0.\dot{3}$	33.$\dot{3}$%
$\frac{3}{5}$	0.6	60%
$\frac{1}{5}$	0.2	20%

2. 0.25, $\frac{5}{9}$, $\frac{2}{3}$, 84%, $\frac{9}{10}$

Page 19 Using a calculator
1. a) 11   b) 24   c) 11
2. a) 14   b) 2   c) 23
3. 1.52×10^6

Page 21 Rounding
1. 6.49   2. 12.06   3. 9.5
4. 1200   5. 1000
6. a) 270   b) 7290 c) 1470   d) 25 350

Page 23 Estimates & checking calculations
1. a) 110   b) 10   c) 909
2. 10 rolls of wallpaper
3. 9 coaches

4. £4.75

Page 25 Ratio
1. a) 4 : 5   b) 1 : 2   c) 5 : 2
2. £200, £300
3. 750 g
4. £2.76
5. Small tin of tuna

Pages 26–27 Answers to practice questions
1. a) 92   b) 407   c) 3060
2. a) Units   b) Tens   c) Tens
   d) Thousands
3. Three million, two hundred and forty-eight thousand and twenty.
4. a) 27, 379, 428, 787, 6394, 6492
   b) 12, 478, 487, 496, 527, 793, 1348
5.

×	2	9	4
6	12	54	24
3	6	27	12
5	10	45	20

6. a) 6512   b) 4181   c) 22 813 d) 215
7. 15°C
8. a) 60   b) 60   c) 130   d) 100
   e) 300   f) 1400   g) 7000   h) 9000
9. a) 4, 8, 12   b) 2, 3, 5, 7, 11
   c) 1, 2, 3, 6, 12
10. $2 \times 2 \times 2 \times 3 = 2^3 \times 3$
11. a) ±10   b) 36   c) ±6   d) 8
12. 2.76×10^9
13. a) $x = 24$ b) $y = 25$ c) $z = 152$
14. 12%
15. 1404p or £14.04
16. 18 tins
17. a) −5   b) −1   c) −12   d) 7
18. £38.25
19. 600
20. 36 cm
21. a) $\frac{7}{10}$ b) $\frac{1}{6}$ c) $\frac{3}{16}$
22. a) 12.69   b) 28.76   c) 2.94
23.

Fraction	Decimal	Percentage
$\frac{1}{4}$	0.25	25%
$\frac{5}{8}$	0.625	62.5%
$\frac{2}{3}$	$0.\dot{6}$	66.$\dot{6}$%

24. 0.274, $\frac{4}{7}$, 61%, $\frac{9}{10}$, 0.93, 94%

Algebra
Quick test answers
Page 29 Algebra 1
1. $S = 3P + 1$
2. a) $n + 6$ b) $p - 4$ c) $3y + 6$
   d) $\frac{h}{7}$ e) $\frac{n}{p} - 5$

Page 31 Algebra 2
1. a) $10a$ b) $6a + 3b$ c) $5xy$
   d) $10ab$ e) $12a^2$ f) $6a + b$
2. Card C
3. a) 13.2   b) −26   c) −25.2

Page 33 Equations 1
1. $x = 5$
2. $x = 6$

3. $x = \frac{7}{4}$ or $1\frac{3}{4}$
4. $x = 2$
5. $x = 4$
6. $x = -1$
7. $x = -1.4$

Page 35 Equations 2
1. $x = 4.6$
2. a) $12x + 2 = 74$
   b) $x = 6$ ∴ length = 34, width = 3

Page 37 Number patterns & sequences
1. a) $2n + 3$ b) $4n - 1$ c) $3n + 5$
2. 2, 1

Page 39 Coordinates & graphs
1. A = (3, 2), B = (1, 4), C = (−2, 1),
   D = (−5, 0), E = (−3, −4), F = (2, −2)
2. a), b) See figure.
   c) $y = 4x$ is steeper than $y = 2x$.
      They both pass through the origin.
   d) See figure.

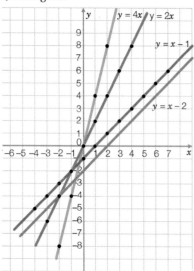

Page 41 More graphs

x	−3	−2	−1	0	1	2	3
y	19	9	3	1	3	9	19

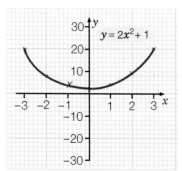

Page 43 Using linear graphs
1. a) 20 mph
   b) Staying stationary
   c) 40 mph

Pages 44–45 Answers to practice questions
1. a) 8 b) 13 c) 32 d) 4
2. a) True b) False c) True
3. a) 8 b) 21 c) 12 d) 50
4. a) $r + 5$ b) $y - 7$ c) $\frac{p}{4}$ d) $\frac{r - 4}{s}$
5. a) $6a$ b) $2x + 3y$ c) $2cd$
   d) $15pr$ e) $20x^2$ f) $4p + 5q$
6. $8a + 10b + 5$
7. a)

n	1	2	3	4	5	6
p	6	10	14	18	22	26

   b) $p = 4n + 2$
8. a) 4 b) 0 c) 17 d) 6
9. a) 320 b) 900
10. a) $4n + 8$ b) n^2
    c) $2n - 2$ d) $4n + 2$
11. a) $n = 16$ b) $n = 6$ c) $a = 1$
    d) $n = 35$
12. a), b) and d)

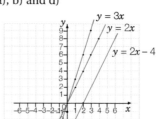

   c) $y = 3x$ is steeper than $y = 2x$, since it has a bigger
      gradient
13. a) $n = 3$ b) $n = -5$ c) $n = -14$
14. a) $4n + 10$ b) $4n + 10 = 22$, $n = 3$
15. $2n + 3$
16. a) $5(x + 3)$ b) $6(x - 2)$
    c) $4(3x + 5)$
17. a) Gradient = 4; intercept = (0, 10)
    b) Gradient = −2; intercept = (0, 6)
18. a) 66.6. mph b) 1 hour
    c) 50 mph d) 1442

Shape, space and measures
Quick test answers

Page 47 Shapes
1. Hexagon
2. See information.

Page 49 Solids
1.

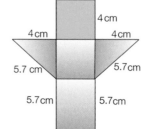

2.

plan

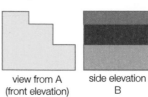

view from A   side elevation
(front elevation)   B

Page 50 Symmetry
1.

2. Plane, rotational, reflective

3. There is another plane at right angles to this one.

Page 51 Constructions & LOGO
1. Forward 2, Turn right 90°, Forward 5, Turn right 90°, Forward 2, Turn right 90°, Forward 5

Page 53 Angles & tessellations
1. a) $a = 140°$ b) $x = 40°$, $y = 90°$
   c) $a = 100°$, $b = 80°$, $c = 80°$
   d) $a = 50°$, $b = 130°$, $c = 50°$, $d = 50°$
2. a) 60°   b) 120°

Page 55 Bearings & scale drawings
1. a) 110°   b) 240°   c) 320°
2. a) 290°   b) 060°   c) 140°

Page 57 Transformations

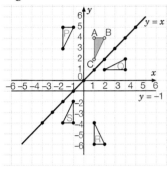

Page 59 Measures & measurement 1
1. 6.2 kg
2. 42 mm
3. 10.5 pints (approximately)
4. A = 9.2 B = 9.5 C = 2.42 D = 2.46
   E = 2.48 F = 6.25 G = 6.75
5. c) 3 kg

Page 61 Measures & measurement 2
1. 0912
2. 180 seconds
3. 0955
4. a) 1832 b) 0827 c) 0234   d) 2136

Page 63 Area & perimeter of 2D shapes
1. a) 27 cm²   b) 36 cm²   c) 44 cm²
   d) 19.6 cm²
2. 30.8 cm (1 dp)

Page 65 Volume of 3D shapes
1. a) 573.7 cm³ b) 96.6 cm³
   c) 3240 cm³
2. 3 cm

Pages 66–67 Answers to practice questions
1. West
2. 300
3. a) 0843   b) 1930   c) 2340   d) 0304
4. 8:35 am
5. 12 edges
6. a) mm   b) kg   c) m
   d) ml   e) m
7. A = 8.4, B = 9.0, C = 0.02, D = 0.06,
   E = 0.08, F = 6.25, G = 6.75
8. a)

   b) 2
9. a) order 1 or no rotational symmetry
   b) order 4
   c) order 2
10. acute: 41°, 72°, 83°

   obtuse: 127°
   reflex: 241°, 379°
   right-angles: 90°
11. i) $a = 80°$
    ii) $b = 155°$
    iii) $c = 138°$, $d = 42°$
    iv) $e = 65°$
    v) $f = 102°$
    vi) $g = 60°$, $h = 60°$, $i = 120°$
12. 14 cm³
13. a) 3750 g   b) 5.3 cm
    c) 4 litres (approx.)
14.

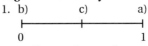

    plan   elevation   elevation
               from A   from B
15. a) 15 cm²   b) 17.5 cm²
    c) 44 cm²
16. a) 68.0 cm²   b) 63.6 cm²
    c) 63.6 cm²   d) 208 cm²
17. 30.8 (1 dp)
18. 17.6 cm² (1 dp)
19. a) 115°   b) 253°   c) 145°
20.

21. a) 30.0 cm³   b) 1750 cm³

Quick test answers
Page 69 Collecting data

Food type	Tally	Frequency

2.

20	6 9	
21	3 4 5	
22	2 7	
23	1 7 9	
24	1 3 6	Stem = 10

Key: 20|6 = 206

Page 71 Representing information
   a) 480   b) 360   c) 600

Page 73 Scatter diagrams & misleading graphs
1. a) As the temperature increases, more ice lollies are sold (positive correlation).
   b) As the temperature increases, fewer cups of tea are sold (negative correlation).

Page 75 Averages 1
1. Mean = 3.7 (1 dp), median = 4, mode = 5, range = 6
2. 4.2 (1 dp)
3. 4

Page 77 Averages 2
1. a) 1.83 sisters (2 dp) b) 1 sister
2. 1.9

Page 79 Probability 1
1. b)   c)   a)
   ├───────────────┼──────────────┤
   0   1

2. a) $\frac{3}{17}$ b) $\frac{4}{17}$ c) $\frac{7}{17}$ d) 0   e) $\frac{17}{17} = 1$

3. 0.68

Page 81 Probability 2

1. 70

2.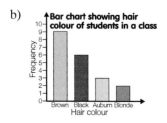

Die 1	6	6	12	18	24	30	36
	5	5	10	15	20	25	30
	4	4	8	12	16	20	24
	3	3	6	9	12	15	18
	2	2	4	6	8	10	12
	1	1	2	3	4	5	6
		1	2	3	4	5	6
				Die 2			

a) $\frac{4}{36} = \frac{1}{9}$ b) $\frac{15}{36} = \frac{5}{12}$

3. red/green, red/black, green/black

Pages 82–83 Answers to practice questions

1. a)

Pictogram showing hair colour

Brown 👁👁👁👁👁
Black 👁👁👁👁
Auburn 👁👁
Blonde 👁

b) Bar chart showing hair colour of students in a class

2.

b		a		c
0		0.5		1

5. a) 67 b) 50 c) 83

6. a) $\frac{2}{11}$ b) $\frac{2}{11}$ c) $\frac{3}{11}$

7. a) $\frac{4}{9}$ b) $\frac{2}{9}$ c) $\frac{5}{9}$ d) 0

8. mean = 3.7 (1 dp), median = 4, mode = 5, range = 6

9. mean = 1.34 sisters (2 dp)

10. 68% = 0.68

11. $\frac{7}{9}$

12. a) Positive correlation: the better you did in test 1 the better you did in test 2.
    b) Approximately 35

13. 140 people

14. a) $\frac{16}{31}$ b) $\frac{10}{14} = \frac{5}{7}$

15. Your opinion that you only want swimming lessons on a Saturday morning is evident.

16. 0.4 × 0.4 = 0.16

Pages 84–86 Answers to practice questions

1. Wednesday

2. £180

3. a) ml (millilitres)
   b) kg (kilograms)
   c) km (kilometres)

4. a) 371 b) 18 c) 459

5. A = (4, 2), B = (2, 4), C = (4, 6);
   D should be at (6, 4)

6. 9°C

7. a) hard = $\frac{15}{28}$ b) soft = $\frac{13}{28}$
   c) mint = 0

8. Rotational symmetry order 4

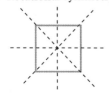

9. a) $s + 4$ b) $2s$ c) $\frac{s + 4}{2}$

10. a) $x = 6$ b) $x = 6$

11. i) $a = 75°$ $b = 105°$
    ii) $c = 123°$
    iii) $d = 73°$ $e = 107°$

12. a) 38 454 b) 27

13. $\frac{8}{15}$

14. Because 4 takes up half of the available space.
    Hence P(4) = $\frac{1}{2}$

15. Pie chart should be drawn with the following angles:
    Cheese = 105°, Salt 'n' vinegar = 150°, Beef = 90°, Smoky bacon = 15°

16. £28

17. $3n + 4$

18. 58.5 cm³ (1 dp)

19. £55 000, £70 000

20.

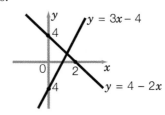

$y = 3x - 4$: gradient = 3,
intercept = (0, –4)
$y = 4 - 2x$: gradient = –2,
intercept = (0, 4)

21. 64.2

22. 1.2 (1 dp)

23. $x = 2.9$ (1 dp)

Index